GW01079949

101 WAYS TO GROW YOUR BUSINESS WITH BARTER

A GUIDE TO THRIVING IN THE 90'S AND BEYOND

KIRK WHISLER & JIM SULLIVAN

WPR Publishing
Books That Make You Think

DEDICATION

This book is dedicated to the tens of thousands of business people around the world who have found that barter is an excellent way to grow their business, increase their profitability, and enjoy a richer personal life. Through their trades of $50, $5,000 and $5,000,000 an industry has developed. These pioneers, and the barter organizations that they have worked with, have laid the foundation for an industry that will affect millions of businesses in the near future.

Library of Congress Catalog Card Number: 96-90389

ISBN 1-889379-01-8

WPR Publishing
Books That Make You Think
3445 Catalina Drive
Carlsbad, CA 92008
619-433-0090

INTRODUCTION

Over the past decade we have done hundreds of thousands of dollars worth of trades. Some of it as direct trades, some through retail barter organizations, some with corporate trading companies, and some with businesses in other countries. We joined our first retail trade organization in 1978. It was not a fruitful experience—and that exchange no longer exists. That same year we did our first trade with a corporate barter company. That experience was a good one, and we still trade with that same company—SGD International.

We have had some major success getting items that have helped our business grow. We also have been burnt more than once. And you can be sure that we would do it all again because we have discovered that barter is a great way of doing business that just gets better every year as the industry matures.

Before I purchased my first new car I bought a book on how to buy a new car. I wanted to make sure I knew the right questions to ask—and what answers to expect. In the case of buying a car I had the alternative of talking with family or friends about the topic. In the case of barter I strongly feel that for every business currently involved in trading there are another 10 to 20 who are not involved because there is no objective voice to help them know if the information that they are hearing about barter is correct. It is our hope that this book will help provide an objective voice to help you discover the advantages—and disadvantages—of barter.

Think of the barter industry as a kid that is about 8 years old (my oldest son, Spencer, happens to be 8). He's old enough to be interesting to talk with and to do things with—but as each year goes by we can do so many more activities with him. The barter industry as it functions now has only existed for a very few decades and is still very much a child. But it is showing enough true promise that we are projecting by the year 2020 a minimum of 20% of all U.S. businesses will be involved in organized barter in one way or another.

We readily admit that we do not know everything there is to know about trading—but we have yet to meet the person who truly does. Like the barter industry, we view this publication as a work in progress and welcome your input.

GETTING BUSINESS

We have found tens of thousands of potential customers across the United States for our products and services. Through our own marketing efforts we are only able to reach a fraction of those potential customers. Through our working with various barter organizations across the U.S. we have added thousands new customers—on both a trade and cash basis.

We view organized barter as one of the most effective ways to get new customers for your products and services—with little or no effort on your part. We have sold numerous pages of advertising in our magazine, *MEXICO Events & Destinations*, with little more than an online ad within the ITEX Internet system.

SPENDING YOUR TRADE

With most exchanges we work with we have found it relatively easy to put together work related trades. In terms of office overhead, we have paid our rent, phone bill, office supplies, equipment repair, and security system fees. We have gotten computers, a color scanner, software, and trade show displays. We have traded for hotels, restaurants, and even airfare. We have done printing, direct mail pieces, print and radio ads. We have gotten accounting and legal services. On a personal basis, I even got the car I drive on trade. Don't expect to get this wide a variety of services as you begin trading. It takes experience and time to work the more interesting deals.

POINT SYSTEM — +

Our original plans called for us to share with you 101 ways to help grow your business with barter. We didn't think that goal would be difficult to reach since barter fits in so nicely with the way we do business as publishers. Having been active barterers for the past ten years and members of numerous barter exchanges over the same period, barter has become a natural way of doing business for us.

We're happy to report we actually ended up with 135 reasons, with the first two listed in this introduction.

Whenever possible we have used the actual comments of the barter exchange personnel and other traders we have contacted. It should give you a better insight into the industry to hear the thoughts of these barter professionals.

The bottom line is not merely doing trades, but ultimately discovering ways to make your current cash revenues go further. If trading is not allowing you to conserve more of your current cash revenues, then something is wrong and you should rethink your approach to barter.

One final thought. We know that this one book hasn't covered all the aspects of retail trade that need to be covered. We look forward to your thoughts on how the next edition of this book could be better.

THANKS

First of all we would like to thank the over 70 barter professionals from across the United States and Canada who have shared their thoughts on how the barter industry can help small business grow successfully. This book would not have been possible without their input.

We would also like to thank Nancy Gillespie for her solid efforts on transcribing certain materials and Kathy Díaz for her care and professionalism in proofing.

On a personal basis, Kirk Whisler would like to thank his brother, Mark, a Sacramento, California, financial planner, for all the excellent business advice he has offered over the years. He would also like to thank his wife, Magdalena, and their three sons, Spencer Diego, Tito Andrés, and Zeke Emilio, for their patience while their Father has been learning about barter. The barter industry does take time to learn, but the results can certainly help enrich business and personal lives.

Jim Sullivan would like to thank Lisa, Leslie and Phil—his Houston Connection— as well as Javier and Felipe for their support and most of all their friendship over the years.

CONTENTS

WHAT BARTER CAN DO FOR YOU

"The number one reason is for new business. In our corporate statement, it says: To increase client sales, to enhance their business and personal lives. Conserving cash flow and bringing cash flow savings to a profit at the end of the year. Basically, that's it. It's a marketing method for bringing in new clients you just don't have now. I think that's a powerful enough reason."

Steve White
President of Cascade Trade Association, Inc.
Seattle, Washington

In this section we will discuss reasons why you should consider trading in general. Tom McDowell, the executive director of the National Association of Trade Exchanges (NATE) discusses why you should do your trading as a member of a trade exchange. "Everybody barters on their own. Most small businesses have done it forever. What an organized barter company does for a business is it alleviates the necessity for a business owner to go out and put his own deals together and get into the barter business. He has his own business to run. So, for a small nominal fee, he can hire a professional to handle his barter transactions for him. It's the same reason most businesses today don't do their own accounting, their own legal work. When you can hire professionals who can do a better job than you, why not put your efforts in the business you know."

There are many reasons to get involved in the barter industry. The 12 we've outlined here are very general. Once you've learned more about the trade business and become a trader yourself, we're sure you'll develop your own specific rationale for continuing to trade.

12 REASONS TO TRADE

1. INCREASE YOUR COMPANY'S PROFITABILITY

One of the easiest ways to increase profits is by lowering overhead. Barter can help you on the way to achieving this seemingly impossible yet desirable objective if, instead of reaching for the telephone book and your checkbook every time a typical business expense comes up, you think trade first.

Rachel Taylor, of Barter Systems, San Antonio, Texas, explains that bartering gives you, "immediate access to a network of other businesses. The bottom line for any business owner is the profit. So if we can help them with their expenses, that's going to increase their bottom line. It doesn't matter how you get there."

For example, as a member of a barter organization, your next small printing job—sales brochure, business cards, stationary, envelopes, flyers, etc.—can easily be given to any one of several print shops in your area that are also members and accept barter in payment for their services. In addition, everything from janitorial services, to copy and fax machine supplies and repairs, to the hotel your sales-people stay at on their next out of town business trip can be "trad-ed for" with a little imagination.

Throughout this book we'll hear from a lot of professionals involved in the barter industry. Franklin Andrade, publisher of *La Oferta Newspaper* in San Jose, California, gives us the perspective of a businessman who uses barter in his everyday business. "I belong to five trade exchanges here in San Jose. I use them to get basic printing, other office supplies, and to keep advertisers happy. I take the trade so I can make a new sale. It helps me bring in new customers. The other benefit of barter is that I've gotten items through exchanges and then sold the item for cash. Trade is the sweetener that has helped our business grow."

The bottom line is you've got better things to spend your cash on (i.e., unfortunately, the U. S. Post Office is still not a member of any barter organization, nor does the IRS accept trade dollars).

2. CREATE A NEW CUSTOMER BASE

Trading introduces you to customers who might otherwise never use your products or services. When they are in need of a particu-lar product or service, these consumers consult their barter club directory or trade broker either before, after or instead of looking in the phone book, listening to radio spots or browsing newspaper ads. Let's say consumer X with a cracked windshield is a member of a particular barter organization and happens to see your adver-tisement in the newspaper for a special on windshield replace-ment. The first thing Mr. X does is check with his barter club for a similar company and a comparable price in trade. You had better have a "too good to be true" promotion running if you expect that customer to call you and spend cash rather than use his trade cred-its elsewhere.

Trading can also open up a new cash customer base as your new trading partners spread positive word of mouth on your business, products and services to their non-bartering friends and especial-ly to their own cash customers. Byron Lester, president of

Merchant Trade in Waco, Texas, refers to this last aspect in his list of the benefits of joining a trade organization. "Primarily, the top reasons for people to join barter would be the increased business. The second reason would be just for improving one's bottom line, because as a result of that supplemental business, you're able to turn around and offset personal and business expenses, thus freeing up cash you can use for other things you can't barter for. Third, we found that through your barter customers, you get cash referrals. So I guess those are three good reasons."

Steve White, president of Cascade Trade Association, Inc. of Seattle, WA, puts it this way: "The number one reason is for new business. In our corporate statement, it says: To increase client sales, to enhance their business and personal lives. Conserving cash flow and bringing cash flow savings to a profit at the end of the year. Basically, that's it. It's a marketing method for bringing in new clients you just don't have now. I think that's a powerful enough reason."

3. You've Got Excess, Slow Moving or Old Inventory 5

Paul Suplizio, the chief executive officer of the International Reciprocal Trade Association (IRTA) summed up what can go wrong with inventory in his speech before the American Association of Advertising Agencies in March of 1994. "Inventory can become excess when new models are brought into the marketplace. New technology may be introduced, making the old technology less desirable. A new color scheme may prove to be more popular than the last one. A new attitude on the part of the consumer toward a product can affect demand. Seasonal miscalculations can have an adverse impact on inventory levels. The holidays may prove bountiful for some products and not others. New product failures are a continuing source of excess inventories. Finally, sagging demand or construction of a new plant can create surplus capacity and spark a need to find new distribution channels for excess output."

For many industries, inventory must be used or moved on a regular, sometimes daily, basis or it is lost forever. The lodging industry is a perfect example of a sector of commerce that has utilized barter to great advantage over the years. If a hotel lets a room go empty for one night, that's lost revenue that cannot be recovered. Most major hotels and hotel chains—and an ever increasing number of smaller independent hotels as well—set aside a percentage of room nights per year for use by various barter organizations. In exchange the hotels receive a variety of hard goods and services. (The overwhelming majority of the trade credits that these hotels accumulate are used for marketing/advertising.

If you've got excess inventory, for whatever reason, you should do some serious investigation into the barter industry. You would be surprised at how many customers for your inventory you will be able to find through barter. Many members of barter organizations never realize just how much they need that 150 yards of carpet until they discover they can get it on trade. If it's just sitting in your storeroom/warehouse taking up space, trade it!

4. KEEP CASH READILY AVAILABLE

Once you become accustomed to trading—where you are always thinking of spending trade dollars rather than your cash—your cash reserves in the bank should automatically increase. As a small business, you try to keep as large a reserve as possible for those unscheduled expenditures or that once in a lifetime deal that happens to come along. But we all know that unfortunately those reserves are usually minimal at best. Perhaps you might work out a formula for depositing so much cash per completed barter transaction into your reserve account. Even 5% of the total amount of each deal would add up sufficiently over time to allow you greater flexibility in dealing with unforeseen circumstances or in taking advantage of that "special" offer. Extending your buying power in this manner is a very real advantage of bartering.

5. EXPAND YOUR CUSTOMER BASE GEOGRAPHICALLY

Let's say you've got a product that could be marketed nationwide if you had the customer base. Creating that base can be an expensive proposition whether you do it through national advertising (creative costs/media expenditures) or direct mail (cost of mailing lists, postage etc.). If you're in this situation then maybe a large franchised retail club with offices in many cities is your best bet.

The networking and marketing potential within such an exchange can provide you with enough distribution outlets to possibly force you to step up production. Harold Rice of the American Exchange Network in Kansas City, Missouri, lists this as one of his top three reasons for trading. "To increase market share, get new customers, and to penetrate markets they would not otherwise have been able to penetrate."

6. IMPROVE MARKETING/ADVERTISING EFFORTS

In relating his reasons why you should consider trading Bruce Kamm, of the ITEX office in New York City, brings up the advertising angle: "Of course the obvious reason is to conserve cash and to improve cash flow. The offspring of it is to bring in additional cash business by using trade dollars to do advertising and marketing."

You can drastically reduce your advertising expenditures through the use of the media that is readily available through local and national barter networks. Space in newspapers and magazines and time on radio and TV are some of the most often bartered commodities. You would be surprised at how many of the ads for well known national companies that appear in popular national magazines are either placed by a barter organization, or the magazine and the advertiser have entered into their own barter arrangement. The same premise holds for electronic media as well—especially radio. Of all media, radio has probably been the most creative and opportunistic when it comes to trading air time. The tourism board of Brazil once traded for $40 million worth of media to promote tourism to Brazil with most of the transaction paid for with hotel rooms. Campaigns are created, and promotions—many times involving two, three or more clients—are completed with barter the sole method of compensation.

In addition, you may improve the quality of your advertising and execute a professional, effective media buy through the use of the creative efforts and media expertise that is available at many barter organizations—an expense that until now you might have thought was out of your reach. If your barter organization does not offer this service, the media itself will often tradeout not only the cost of ad placement, but the cost of creating your ad as well. If you're always thinking trade you're more apt to come up with innovative ways to trade.

For more on advertising, marketing and media see the "Media Services" section in chapter 4, *Products & Services.*

7. IMPROVE STAFF MORALE AND PRODUCTIVITY

Sometimes in the hectic pace and uncertainty of today's economy, little things that fall under the column of good business sense are put aside until better times. Items such as providing incentives and/or bonuses to your employees are often the first to be cut. You know how valuable bonuses are to staff morale. You also know how your staff responds positively to incentives with renewed dedication and in the long run with improved productivity. Barter provides you with the means of cost-effectively initiating an incentive or promotions program. If you don't think you can afford to send your top salesperson of the quarter to Acapulco for a week, you're not thinking barter.

Sometimes not only incentives and bonuses are paid with barter but partial salaries as well. A business may have a membership in a trade exchange and have separate sub-accounts for their employees. The employees gets to spend and the accounting goes to the employer. Steve Goldbloom, president, Bay Area and Hawaii Barter Exchange, San Francisco, California, is one supporter of this system: "We have one account that has 62 card holders."

8. IMPROVE THE QUALITY OF YOUR HOME LIFE

Spending the barter credits you earn through your business for items you might need at home is one of the pleasures of bartering. Use barter to provide your family with those little "luxuries" you have been putting off and you'll experience the bonus pleasure that comes with the realization that your business has provided the opportunity to directly improve the quality of life for you and your family. How would your house look with new wall to wall carpeting? Or, maybe it's time for that satellite dish you've been thinking about for years.

9. Barter Is Becoming A Major Industry

You need to use all the resources that are open to you to stay ahead in today's business environment. Barter is a resource that is being used by an ever increasing number of credible companies to gain a competitive edge. If you think bartering is a tool used mainly by marginal companies trying to stay afloat, consider the multi-million dollar empty office building that Citicorp, the national banking concern, traded for advertising credits; or the $10 million dollars worth of nuts and bolts that defense industry giant McDonnell Douglas traded a few years ago for trade credits that were used for, among other items, rental cars and hotel rooms.

The estimated 400,000 companies that bartered billions of dollars worth of goods and services through retail and corporate trade companies last year—many of them well known Fortune 500 corporations—are making the most of every resource available to them. Can you afford to do any less?

10. Barter Creates Its Own Unique Economy

There are many businesses in the barter environment that enjoy what Joe Hill of Trade Club Exchange in Orange County, California, refers to as "a reverse economy." In this situation you end up putting in more effort spending the barter dollars/credit you build up from sales than into the sales effort itself. You would be surprised at how many products and services fall into this category. Don't get the wrong idea. We're not saying it's that difficult to find ways to spend your barter credits. Try giving a few barter checks or your barter credit card to your spouse, girlfriend or kids for an afternoon, then stand back and learn the true meaning of "creative spending." But you'll have to admit it would be nice if you could get this "reverse economy" thing going in your everyday business.

Douglas Dagenais, vice president of Barter Corp., in Oakbrook Terrace, Illinois has other ideas on the uniqueness of the barter economy. "The concept of barter as a method of payment creates a new market dynamic that otherwise may not be there on a cash basis. It creates a new motivation of payment. That motivation of payment creates new customers, new customers create incremental business for the vendors. Incremental business has reduced costs. And you're buying with idle assets, non-performing assets. The key is to implement it effectively within your business so you make sure you are, in fact, using a non-performing asset and that you are, in fact, selling to an incremental market."

Nelson Guyer, the President of San Diego Barter offers his views on barter economy. "We're going to expand your base, we're going to increase your profits, and we're going to reduce your cash outgo. You're going to be put into the advantageous position of being able to access thousands of goods and services at your cost of your service. And remember, your cost of your service or product includes a profit margin. So your profit margin is inverted to become your buying discount in our network."

There's a variety of ways to look at how a barter economy works. You know your business better than anyone else. You are the best judge of how to make it work for your company.

11. USE BARTER FOR INVESTMENTS

Once you've accumulated any significant amount of barter credits, you may want to explore the idea of turning those credits into cash. At this stage of barter's development it is possible to make substantial investments with barter. Ryan Van Trees of BXI of Santa Barbara and Ventura, California, couldn't be more emphatic when asked his main reasons for someone joining a barter organization: "Profit, profit, profit and more profit." He then added another good point in the same vein. "Look, in barter you've got the opportunity to use trade dollars to do some real hard dollar investments in real estate, stocks or antiques. Whatever. The profits you make on those investments are in cash."

Don Schmidt, ITEX San Diego agrees with Mr. Van Trees: "After someone has traded first of all for replacement of business expenses, secondly for personal perks like travel and restaurants, they should consider the third area of barter—making long term investments. These can include real estate, stocks and other investments purchased with barter."

12. Donate Barter Credits ⓮

Barter credits are perfect for donating because most non-profit organizations and churches are always short on revenues. While it may sometimes be hard for you to donate cash to your favorite cause, and since that cause might not need whatever excess inventory you have, you could consider a barter donation. That non-profit would have little problem finding dozens of things to spend the barter on: a direct mail campaign or to fix a leaky roof.

2

WHAT IS TRADE ?

*" I think the most significant event in
the barter industry was in 1982, when we
were recognized as third-party record keepers.
That Tax Fiscal Act legitimized the business for
the first time. No longer did people have
the perception that people traded to evade taxes.
There is not any real tax advantage to trade. The
advantages are the new business that you receive
and the cash that you conserve by using the trade
that you earned to offset normal cash expenses."*

Scott Whitmer
President of The Exchange in Orlando, Florida
and current President of the
International Reciprocal Trade Association (IRTA)

7 KEY POINTS IN THE HISTORY OF TRADE

1. BARTER WAS THE FIRST REAL COMMERCE 15

When man first started interacting with his fellow man he had only trading or bartering as a means of exchanging goods. These direct trades might have involved trading a recently killed deer for a basket of corn. Even when currencies came into common use, much of commerce was still done on a trade basis. When the United States was founded we had numerous currencies. Every state had their own currency, none of the same value. Business books of the time helped educate business people on what one state's currency was worth compared with others. In fact, business books through the mid-1800s talked as much about trading between businesses as they did about one business purchasing from another.

In many currently developing Third World countries, direct trade is still an important aspect of daily commerce. Timothy Ritchie of Merchant Trade Inc., in Dallas, Texas offers his views on early barter: "The key point was when somebody traded a saber-toothed tiger leg for a pile of firewood or something warm to keep the cold off. Barter is an innate method of exchange that has been in existence since history, since there were thinking people who had needs. You'll find in many parts of the world barter is essentially the only medium of exchange. Even though there are shells and rocks and carved items that are exchanged, a lot of times it's a pig for a dozen eggs, a chicken for a pot or a pan, piece of clothing, etc. These people don't actually have any money."

2. THE BIRTH OF MODERN RETAIL TRADING   16

It is generally agreed that the modern retail barter industry was started in 1960 by former banker Marvin "Mac" McConnell. The organization that he started in North Hollywood, California, would later become Barter Exchange International (BXI), one of the largest retail barter organizations in the world.

During the early days of the retail barter industry, trade exchanges were started by both honorable business people and by those look-ing to make a quick buck. The honorable business people were looking to be part of an industry that they felt would grow to become an important part of the economy. Many of these people went on to help form the International Reciprocal Trade Association (IRTA) in 1979, the first important industry trade asso-ciation (For more on IRTA see page 116). IRTA would take on as one of its major goals the professionalizing of the barter industry.

At the same time, those looking to make a fast buck off of an unde-veloped industry were promising everything under the sun to get clients to sign up. During the 1970s and early 1980s, hundreds of barter exchanges started up, signed up members and in a matter of months or a few years the exchange was gone, often leaving mem-bers owed thousands of dollars.

3. THE TAX EQUITY AND FISCAL RESPONSIBILITY ACT

Before the Tax Equity and Fiscal Responsibility Act (TEFRA), retail barter was definitely an underground economy. Certain barter organizations openly told members that trade was a way of getting around paying taxes. The International Reciprocal Trade Association took the stand that the industry needed to become legally recognized by the government as a viable form of com-merce.

The result was the Tax Equity and Fiscal Responsibility Act that was signed into law by President Reagan in 1982. The key item of TEFRA was that it recognized barter exchanges as third-party record keepers—a status similar to banks and accountants. It also required exchanges to annually report to the Internal Revenue Service the barter income of their members. This is done on 1099 forms. The third area that TEFRA covered prohibited the IRS from auditing barter members merely because they belonged to a barter organization.

Duncan Banner, area director of BXI in San Diego on barter and the IRS: "The IRS did studies in the late 70s, early 80s, to determine if typical taxpayers who belong to barter companies are any more inclined to be defrauding the government than any other group of taxpayers. The finding was no, they're not, which has in essence protected the industry from tax audits ever since that study was done. Significant. In fact, it seems barter owners and clients get audited no more and no less than anybody else, because their own studies showed there's not a lot of difference."

Scott Whitmer, president of The Exchange in Orlando, Florida and current president of the International Reciprocal Trade Association (IRTA), offers his views on the importance of the passage of this law: "I think the most significant event in the barter industry was in 1982, when we were recognized as third-party record keepers. That Tax Fiscal Act legitimized the business for the first time. The rumors from accountants that there were IRS barter projects that were taking place were eliminated, and it really cleaned up the industry. No longer did people have the perception that people traded to evade taxes."

The importance of this law is underscored by Chris Haddawy of Barter Business Network in Reno, Nevada: "With 1099s for the barter industry, which happened about 14 years ago, the government recognized trade as a legitimate form of doing business saying, 'Okay, as long as it's all above board.' That was a big step in the history of barter."

Bruce Kamm, ITEX, New York City also views TEFRA as important. "The TEFRA Act legitimatized the barter industry. It recognized us as a viable banking institution with the IRS. It became a situation now where it's no longer a red flag if you're doing barter and it's something the IRS likes, because they're getting paid taxes on barter transactions. With ITEX the 1099s are all magnetically recorded and we get thank-you letters from the IRS."

Don Mardak, the president of Continental Trade Exchange, in New Berlin, WI, agrees. "Credibility was introduced through the passage of the TEFRA Act of 1982. The government recognized in America that barter was a taxable event and it brought credibility to the whole industry."

4. COMPUTERS

As most of us now realize, computers help us do our business faster and better. It allows many industries to grow more rapidly than they would other wise.

Because of the complex nature of barter transactions—you have three entities involved: the buyer, the seller, and the exchange—most professionals within the industry agree barter could not have grown as it has without computers.

Mark Tracy, president of American Commerce Exchange in Toluca Lake, CA, remembers the early days before computers. "When we first started, I had a little old lady who would debit and credit our accounts in accounting books. At the end of the month, I had two ladies who would get out the Selectric II typewriters and type up the statements. From there, we went to a system where we had a computer terminal in our office feeding into another system. The problem was you lose control. If there are any problems, you had to reconcile it the following month. It was a very bad system. Then we had a single user system called the PAB, which was really good. You had the control, but you could only have one person use it at a time. Now we have legitimate technology. It's like going from a Volkswagen to a Jaguar."

Tom McDowell, executive director of NATE, agrees on how computers helped advance barter. "I think the real start of barter was the result of the advent of the personal computer, because it made the accounting system feasible for small businesses to get into."

The importance of the computer as an advancement in the history of barter is widely held. Listen to these other barter professionals:

Jack Schacht, president of Illinois Trade Association: "Computers made barter what it is today. We wouldn't have been able to do this without computer technology. That added to the power of this ideal concept which allows businesses to tap into resources, inventories, downtime, or empty hotel rooms and use it as currency. A very powerful concept. Now we should make it all work through computer technology by passing trade credits from client to client. I don't think it's ever going to stop."

Susan Williams, president of Barter Connection, in Santa Cruz, CA: "The key point is about 30 years ago computers came on the scene, and it was at that point we became an industry. The record keeping we do could not be done on a ledger—you have to have a computer. A lot of barter occurred before then but it became a far more sophisticated system once computers came on the scene."

Douglas Dagenais, Barter Corp., Oakbrook Terrace, Illinois: "The computer and technology are going to continue to play a big part in making our services more efficient to both us and the client. We're in the information business, and you need technology to get information out quickly and effectively."

Kenneth Meharg, president of Unlimited Business Exchange (UBE), in Malden, MA: "I've been on computers for ten years. The first six years of my business, maybe until 1986, I was either doing it by hand or relying on someone else's computer. But computerization has taken off. Before, we had one little 386, and now I have six 486s floating around the office."

Bob Bagga CTB, vice president, Barter Business Exchange, Toronto: "The growth of the barter industry is due to the evolution of the computer. This service industry would not be where it is if not for technology."

Chris Haddawy, Barter Business Network: "Another thing which we've seen happen over the last four or five years are the types of software that are out their to help run your trade exchange, that helps with travel, and also with the fax back directories. I think if you want to make it in the barter industry today you really need to be on the cutting edge of the technological advances people are using."

Steve White, Cascade Trade: "Communications is what got us to where we are today. Faxes made things a little easier. The PC made it easier, and then communications through modems. It's made it easier for an organization like mine to meet the guys on the East Coast and Los Angeles. With travel and communication opportunities it's enabled us to meet each other and expand our markets. By expanding our markets, we expand our trade credit value and its spendability."

Lisa Peters, Trade Systems Interchange, Redondo Park, CA: "One of the key factors was the advent of computers in so many offices so each individual barter company could run independent of other influences, they could maintain control, have all the record keeping in the data bases, all the tools they needed to run effectively. That would be the most dramatic change over the last 40 or 50 years."

5. THE ECONOMY

Another cornerstone in the growth of the barter industry has been changes in the economy. Traditionally, during downturns in the economy, more businesses turn to trade deals, either direct or through barter organizations of one sort or another.

In recent decades businesses who started bartering during the downturns have continued during the better times. Bob Bagga, Barter Business Exchange, on this key point: "Look at the economic times we are in. We look at the late '80s and early '90s as being a deep recession. Barter was at a point in its growth where both the economy and computerization were crossing each other's path where we could take advantage of both."

Timothy Ritchie, Merchant Trade Inc., reflects on the economic realities of the 1980's: "The key point was probably in the early 1980s, the first really major recession. America's economy had just grown at an incredible pace for a number of years, where cash was king. Cash is still king. It always will be. But all of a sudden there was a shortage for many businesses, and they really started looking at other ways of maintaining their level of business, maintaining their advertising, their lifestyles. Instead of just exchanging cash, they began to exchange goods and services, primarily in a direct manner with the provider of whatever it was they wanted. Then some people who had already begun to develop this concept of being a third party record keeper began to capitalize on that shortage of cash to really get their message out there. Since then, literally hundreds of exchanges have begun to flourish around America and, indeed, around the world, although I'm focusing on the American market here. When money was tight, people reverted to what was natural—to exchange what they had for what they wanted."

Duncan Banner, BXI, on the same subject: "It seems like 15 years ago, people joined because they were doing well and wanted to add a few percent more to their business and spend it on things. But there's been a remarkable surge of people joining in the last few years, not because they're doing well but because they are doing badly, and because they need customers and trade works. So the industry is growing because it does create new customers that you otherwise wouldn't have. That's why we can spend all day, every day, seeing people and talking to them without running a single advertisement."

6. ITEMS AVAILABLE THROUGH BARTER

Every year, a wider selection of the products and services available worldwide are entering into the barter industry. In the early days of the retail barter industry it's safe to say that only around 10% to 20% of the products that you could buy for cash would be available through trade. Today that figure is over 80%. That doesn't mean that they are available through every exchange or available all the time, but the laundry list of services and products is growing rapidly across the industry. Bob Meyers, of *Barter News Magazine* agrees, "I would say it evolves around fulfillment, in other words, the ability to get products and services today is much greater than it was years ago, because more companies are involved in it."

Douglas Dagenais, Barter Corp., on finding items on trade: "I'm a firm believer that once you're committed to something, if you focus on it, you can secure it. We've secured absolutely every product category you can imagine on a trade basis at one time or another. Some of them worked better than others, but we've been able to secure absolutely every commodity at some time or another on a trade basis. It comes down to a matter of focus."

Here's some other industry views on item availability:

Tom McDowell, of NATE: "When they figured out how to make money—they started charging reasonable fees and getting what it took to run a business—then the owners of the exchanges stopped being the biggest consumers of their primary products and started leaving those products for their customers. As more and more products became available, the service level increased and the satisfaction level increased."

Don Mardak, Continental Trade Exchange: "As we've grown, our product choices have grown so significantly that it's hard to believe it's the same business. In fact, who would have believed you could get a long distance service on trade, or you could get computers on trade, because they were very hard to get at one time."

Tom Archibald, National Commerce Exchange, Tampa Bay offers a unique perspective on the use of credit cards and the future of barter: "Many years ago when VISA/MasterCharge first started, there were a few businesses that accepted the VISA or MasterCharge card. There wasn't a whole lot of people who actually had cards, but there was a lot more people who had cards then there were businesses accepting them. What happened over time was that businesses realized that, hey, if I'm not taking that plastic, I'm missing a big part of business out there. The rest is history. You can hardly go anywhere where they don't accept VISA/MasterCharge, Discover, American Express. We are now in a position where businesses need to realize if they're not doing bartering, they are missing a substantial portion of the business that's being done in this country today."

7. THE ENTREPRENEURS

"Entrepreneurs by definition have the courage needed to adapt to change." Michael Caron, president, BarterPlus, Toronto, Canada.

The final, and perhaps most important, cornerstone in the history of barter has been the quality of people who have been attracted to the industry—and have stuck with it. It is safe to say that these pioneers all shared a common entrepreneurial sprit. Duncan Banner, BXI, on the early days of barter: "The industry was started by Mac McConnell in 1960. He had a thrift and loan and banking background. He literally created the necessary software to create the commercial barter industry. He made a lot of money. He took the company public in the 70s." Mike Neal, VP Marketing, ITEX: "I think McConnell, Mac McConnell, the founder of BXI deserves a great deal of credit. I think he did a great job in pioneering a new idea. I have nothing but respect for BXI and what they have done" The creators of the barter organizations were not the only entrepreneurs who were the prime movers behind the growth of barter. There were also the farsighted people who became members. Don Mardak, Continental Trade Exchange, reflects on the spirit of traders: "What I've heard from a couple of other people is that the common bond is an entrepreneurial spirit that really seems to separate them from other business people. Also, they're just a little more—I'd like to use the word "liberal"—in their business thinking. I don't mean liberal versus conservative. They're people who enjoy life. They're people who will go to Las Vegas and enjoy gambling a little bit. They're not just the staid old business person who says, 'I only deal in cash. That's the way I've always done it. My grandfather started the business. He did it that way, and we're not changing.' That kind of mentality is difficult to work with. It has to be somebody who has a willingness to have a life and a lifestyle, to spend money for some personal things as well." Another view was shared by Bob Meyers, Barter News, "I have a real love for the creativity of it and the uniqueness of trade. I never come across something that is quite all-encompassing like this. It doesn't matter really what aspect of a business you're talking about—barter can be applied to it."

The early history of retail barter is littered with the remains of exchanges started by people who only wanted to make a fast buck and really didn't care about the long term future of the industry. The industry is now made up of people who are looking to barter as a career—their profession. Continues Mardak, "Many of us go back far enough to have seen things like the bad press that was given back in 1984, when there was a 20/20 show with Barbara Walters and Hugh Downs crucifying the barter industry. If you've seen that show, you realize they were talking about a different breed of business person. In other words, the first generation of barterers were people that didn't have the format down properly. They were charging trade for their fees instead of cash. Therefore, they had to rake off the system and take merchandise out of it to convert to cash instead of allowing the system to survive on its own right earning cash from the fees. Because of that, most of those people have disappeared." Lois Dale, President, Barter Advantage Inc., New York, adds: "The fact is that more legitimacy has come to the industry, more awareness and better people have been getting into the industry—not the quick scheme people, the con people." Tom McDowell, NATE, offers his perspective: "The thing that really helped to establish the growth of barter was when trade exchange owners realized they still needed cash revenues to run their businesses, that they couldn't run their businesses entirely on barter as many of them tried to do in the early days. Today we've reached the point where professionalism in barter has finally started to take over. When we see exchange owners that now send their sales people and brokers to seminars to get training. I'm proud to say barter is involved to the point now where it's the people that are making the business more than anything else."

Barter Business Network's Chris Haddawy explains how much bartering's image has changed: "15 years ago, barter was a dirty word. It was something that was sort of an underground thing, where now a lot of corporations see it as a legitimate business tool." Nelson Guyer, San Diego Barter, confirms this viewpoint: "I see barter as having attained a degree of respectability and credibility that it has never before attained. Twenty years ago, even 10 years ago, I would never have used I wouldn't have used the term 'barter' in the name of my company. I would have called it what most of the older exchanges do—'exchange,' 'network,' 'trade,'— using any words to circumvent 'barter'. Today I put 'barter' right out there in front—San Diego Barter. That's what we are, that's what we do. A lot of businesses are interested in trade and barter today."

Duncan Banner, BXI, offers his opinions on the growth of the industry: "The other things that are significant are the inception of IRTA and NATE. IRTA came about, I guess, about 15 years ago. Later on, a faction of people who were part of IRTA had a disagreement and formed their own association called NATE. That's a significant happening. The events of the last few years, with ITEX going public, is positive. There's been tremendous coverage in the news as the economy has slumped, pointing out that barter is a wonderful hedge against inflation and protects people in tough times."

Alan Zimmelman, area director for BXI West Los Angeles, on his business philosophy: "I owned and operated a hotel and a bakery in the past and now I want to stay in the barter business. I like to the work. Quality is more important than the size of my exchange. I want to recognize all my clients. That's the success of good customer service." Bob Meyers, Barter News, sums it up: "Barter is a very entrepreneurially driven industry. I think it offers a lot of potential."

5 TYPES OF TRADE ORGANIZATIONS

"I don't know if there are advantages to locally-owned or franchises, except in terms of ownership. Whether you are a franchise or locally-owned company, the quality of the service provided to the client varies in many instances based on the size of the client base that they can tap into. Just because I'm a locally-owned company, I may have a large client base, larger than some national franchises. On the other hand, the national franchise offers flexibility—but not as much as perceived, because most local operators have reciprocal relationships with the exchanges around the country. So in many instances, you can accomplish the same thing through a locally owned company that has reciprocal relationships as you can through a franchise network. It really depends on how strong the client base is and the market that you are working in. It's got nothing to do with ownership." Douglas Dagenais, vice president Barter Corp., Oakbrook Terrace, Illinois.

1. DIRECT TRADES

Nearly every business has done it at one time or another. Your print shop prints a restaurant menu in exchange for meals. A major TV network gets airline tickets in exchange for air time. Direct trades work for most businesses when it drops into your lap—a business you're already dealing with or whose services you can use on a regular basis approaches you about a trade.

There are several major disadvantages to direct trade. First, you have to find someone with a product that you want that also wants something you have. This can take a lot of time and negotiating. Secondly, and perhaps the reason that direct trades don't work for most day to day business expenses, both sides have to get equal value out of the trade.

Zeke Montes, publisher of *Tele Guía de Chicago* states, "We have found that direct trades work best for us. Second best would be to go with one of the prestigious organizations like Illinois Trade, ITEX, or Barter Exchange."

2. RETAIL TRADING ORGANIZATIONS

This is the most common type of barter organization—there are at least 600 of them in the United States. The basic concept is that you earn credits within the organization for services or products that you provide to other members. You can then spend those credits on services and products provided by other members. The barter organization takes a small commission on the deal in order to support their services (see the chapter *Before You Join* for more information on this). Lisa Peters, Trade Systems Interchange, explains it further, "Bartering in an organized network is a win/win situation. They're winning when they get the business, they're winning when they're saving cash, and we're winning when we get paid our 10%—that's how we all make our money. Everyone is benefiting from this."

Members of retail organizations tend to be small businesses owned by people with an entrepreneurial spirit. The average amount traded per member ranges from $200 to $700 per month. The vast majority of these trades are with businesses within 25 miles of the member business. A typically successful organization will have at least 80% of the types of businesses listed in chapter 3 as members.

Trade Club Exchange in Orange County, California is a good example of a recent retail trade start-up. Headed by Joe Hill, the organization started in 1992 with 750 members in its first year. Four years later they have 1,750 active members doing a substantial amount of trading per month.

There are two basic types of Retail Exchanges—Locally-Owned Retail Exchanges and Nationally Managed Retail Exchanges. Here are some of the advantages of each:

Locally-Owned Retail Exchanges

"An independent is able to make his own marketing decisions. That can be good and bad. But the energy you derive by being the owner of your own company far surpasses what a franchise can do for you. Theoretically, a franchise system could be very well run; there just isn't anybody running them like McDonald's or Burger King or Honda. So the advantage is still to the independent exchange because they can get information from an organization like NATE or the IRTA without having to spin 30% off the top to another company just for the billing process. The value of the franchise has gone down, again, because of the ability to go out and buy software or a computer system that was very costly 10 or 12 years ago to create a program to monitor that product's effectiveness. Now anyone can go out and spend less than $15,000 for hardware and software and have top-of-the-line communications software and hardware in their exchange instead of spinning off 30% to a franchise exchange for balancing the credits. If there weren't organizations like NATE, then the franchises would also have more power. NATE members are very pro-active, they're very good at sharing the information they have to educate us vastly more than any of the franchises do." Steve White, Cascade Trade Association.

More than 50% of all barter organizations are independent, locally-owned businesses. The well established ones have been around for 15 years or more and often have 1,000, 2,000 or more members. Their range of services is wide—from minimal for ones just starting up to impressive stores, huge warehouses, and interesting auctions, sales, and mixers for the established, energetic ones.

8 Common Reasons To Go With A Locally-Owned Exchange

A. More Money is Spent Locally

"The biggest difference is the money. Most of the franchises are at 10%. They have to kick back 2.5%, all the way up to 4.5% to the national exchange. In my opinion, there's just not enough money left for that franchisee to go after higher quality personnel to be able to service the account; whereas the independents can charge anywhere from 10 to 15%, and now they can kick back a point or two to their employees and give those employees a real incentive. Also, they're not tied in to corporate, so when I hear that corporate sends out their statements two weeks late, I don't have to worry about that—I'm in control and I don't have to deal with the problems." Mark Tracy, American Commerce Exchange.

Nelson Guyer, San Diego Barter, on his preference for an independent exchange: "There is no distinction between the actual operations of a chain exchange and an independent exchange when it comes right down to operations. The only difference is the ones that are part of a larger corporation do pay 20 to 30% of their income to the franchise, which keeps them from providing as good a service and still derive a fair profit for their efforts. So I am pro independent for that reason. The nature of an exchange is such that it will always be independent, even if you choose to pay a portion of your profits to a central company."

B. CUSTOMER SERVICE

Industry professionals were in agreement on this key point. Francy Naderzad, president of Master Trade in Los Gatos, CA, declares, "Better customer service. If clients have problems, they can call customer service directly and get the service quicker." Harold Rice, American Exchange Network, observes: "Primarily because of the level of service they can get. The independent ones have a little more flexibility and control and can provide a wider range of services than an individual franchisee has at his disposal." Sheryll Moyer, Barter Connection, Santa Cruz: "What I say to people is that I emphasize our customer service, we're really able to help them, a lot more attention is given to them."

C. FLEXIBILITY

"We're unencumbered, number one, and probably in many ways more creative in the way we market our services, in the way we have developed our own software for managing the transactions, and our own methods of communicating with our clients. This is one of the main things. I could see some of the advantages to bigness. However, I notice that because I compete with several large franchises in my marketplace, many of their customers are unhappy with the way they have kind of gotten lost in the size of the operation and communication and availability and knowledge of how and what is available. In that sense, I'm glad we're independent of the many rules and regulations that often come with size." Timothy Ritchie, Merchant Trade Inc.

D. Independence

"It really depends on the person. An entrepreneur is an entrepreneur, and they would not like to join a national exchange; whereas a person who might need a little bit more guidance would join and have a franchiser over them." Lois Dale, president, Barter Advantage Inc., New York.

E. Locally-Owned Exchanges Tend To Be Stronger Than The National Exchanges

"I believe in every single city in this country where there is an independent and a franchise, the independent is the stronger trade exchange, bar none. Every single city. Maybe the franchise as a whole is bigger than any one trade exchange. Because you can go to Chicago, you can go to Los Angeles, you can go to San Francisco, wherever you go, the independent trade exchanges in most cities is stronger than the franchises, so that must tell you there's a reason for that. For one thing, the franchisees don't make as much money as the independents make. If you were to take on a franchise, you're going to make lots of money. It's a fact. Even though they tell you you can now say you're national, you can be national by just affiliating with other trade exchanges. The thing they want most in their community is what a local trade exchange can provide for them. Even though somebody can say, 'We have resorts all over the world,' if somebody isn't into traveling, that isn't going to mean much to them." Don Mardak, Continental Trade Exchange.

F.. Many Can Supply National Services

"If you're a franchise you're stuck doing business with the other franchises in your network. As an independent, you can pick and choose the top exchanges around the country to do business with. So we do business with Barter Corp., Chicago, and Illinois Trade Association, between the two of them they probably have 7,000 accounts. Well, now we have access to 7,000 accounts in the Chicago area. If we were a BBX office, we would be doing business with a BBX office, which maybe has 500 to 600 accounts. Our clients have a big advantage over a BBX client traveling to Chicago." Chris Haddawy, Barter Business Network.

Sheryll Moyer, Barter Connection, agrees, "Through NATE and other reciprocals we can do almost everything for them that a franchise can."

G. THE PERCEPTION THAT NATIONAL EXCHANGES ARE STRONGER MAY BE A MYTH

"If you look back from a historical perspective, 15 years ago the independents were quite fearful of being overtaken by the franchises. Franchises, when I first started *Barter News*, were Exchange Enterprises and Barter Systems, Inc., which were two national franchises that are no longer around. From that perspective, is the fear really there? You know what I mean? I don't see that happening for this reason. I think that this is a very entrepreneurial type of operation, labor intensified, and regional. Sales are really incumbent upon a very motivated individual or company into cookie cutter brokerages on a national scale. While it can be done in hamburgers and a lot of other things, it's much more difficult here. Of course, when you start talking about the franchise concept, one of the real sales tools is the fact that you have national advertising and national uniformity. Certainly you don't have that in the barter business. You have an ITEX or BX in a particular city that has a motivated, dedicated staff that goes out of their way to service the clientele. That doesn't mean that same uniform effort is going to be provided in another city. There is no uniformity. It makes it a lot more difficult." Bob Meyers, *Barter News Magazine*.

H. LOCAL MANAGEMENT

This is perhaps the key point in choosing a locally-owned exchange. Here are some comments from exchange owners on the subject. Bob Bagga, Barter Business Exchange: "From what is available out there right now, the independent has more control and direction of what the company's doing. If there's something a different franchisee does, it can reflect badly on your franchise or the franchiser. So you're not in control of what's happening. Therefore, it can relate badly to your organization. What I'm seeing with the franchises that are out there, is that they're not consistent enough in dealing with their operations. And they're not able to provide the same level of service right across the board. They're not taking as active a role in each individual office as they should."

Another view on the topic of local management comes from Barter Systems' Rachel Taylor: "In our area, businesses do business because they know each other. There is some sort of cliquish thing, skepticism, and they want to do business in a smaller community. They know they can also trade outside of it. But I really think independents manage their accounts better than the franchises. They give more specialized, individual treatment."

Tom McDowell, NATE: "With an independent trade exchange the owner of that business lives in that community, he deals with those business people, he has to face them day in and day out. They're his livelihood, and the energy levels are different than what the franchise people would like to see because they're thousands of miles removed and they're bottom line oriented, not customer service oriented."

Scott Whitmer, The Exchange and IRTA: "Our operation is concentrated locally, as opposed to looking to do business on a nationwide basis. We have a very strong, local, client base. We currently have over 1,350 business owners in central Florida. We reciprocate nationally and internationally with other trade companies, but as opposed to most franchise companies, we are very strong in the local base. A lot of the franchises that we are familiar with may be collectively strong nationally, but usually they don't have a very large, local, client base. We're more focused on our local business owners and their needs."

Lisa Peters, Trade Systems Interchange: "Because we are independent, we have complete control over the activities and policies of our own exchange; therefore, we can decide what is best for our client base. We can set credit terms, set things for the ultimate benefit of us and our clients. That kind of freedom is not present within a franchise operation. I'm not suggesting the franchisers don't work really hard to service their clients. But, frankly, a good chunk of the money is being paid to a distant office in order to do things that are routine in our office, like running statements and doing authorizations. We handle that very effectively and efficiently at a very low cost within our office, so we put our money into broker services so we can provide the best possible communications with our clients so they get maximum benefit from all the opportunities in the exchange. And while I'm sure some franchise operations can do that well, especially some of the bigger ones, on a smaller level, the money just isn't there to hire all the people needed to service the clients."

NATIONALLY-MANAGED RETAIL EXCHANGES

Several hundred of the barter organizations that exist are franchised from a larger organization. The two largest organizations selling franchises are Business Exchange International (BXI), headquartered in Los Angeles; and ITEX, headquartered in Portland, Oregon. Both BXI and ITEX claim over 20,000 members each, and roughly 150 local offices each. Each of the organizations brings very positive elements to the business table. ITEX was one of the first barter organizations to go online, originally operating their own online system and, as of August 1995, shifting to a well thought-out World Wide Web site (http://www.itex.net./). The site offers a detailed listing of ITEX members nationwide by business category, an extensive listing of "Haves" (items that people are looking to trade) and an interesting listing of "Wants" (items people are seeking).

The following story will hopefully demonstrate the impact a site like this can have: Late one Friday afternoon I was meeting with a business person that we have done several projects with. He had some products he wanted to trade so I listed them on the ITEX site. When he got home—a half an hour later—he had already gotten 2 phone calls regarding his listing. Needless to say he was impressed and has become a believer in barter.

BXI also has its strengths: thousands of quality members; well trained barter brokers; and the *BXI HOTLINE*, one of the better barter newsletters. Here are some listings from a recent editios:

> Mac Laptop–Powerbook. 150 w 16/80, 28.8 internal
> modem, database, DTP, software....

Funeral Director—All faiths. Funerals, cremations, burials...
Shipping worldwide....
Waikiki Timeshare–Fully equipped one bedroom. Single
floating week...
San Francisco TV–30 second spots reach 4.5 million in
Oakland, San Jose, San Francisco...
Offset Printing Press–Ryobi 3200-CD. Great for in-house
print shop...
Hot Air Balloon–Fly Napa Valley...
Cabo San Lucas–Stunning view of quaint harbor from your
balcony...

Alan Zimmelman of BXI West Los Angeles, on the strengths of his system: "With BXI you have a strong network that has operated without interruption for 36 years. We stand behind our deals— somethings banks don't always do. Putting in 80 hours a week has made the West Los Angeles BXI a success. The ability to discriminate between erstwhile business people and the rest of the population. We work our clients very hard for their own benefit."

One thing that seems for sure: both BXI and ITEX will be around for years to come. ITEX is a public company and proudly boasts that they are the only barter organization to be publicly traded on NASDAQ. Both organizations are definitely in growth modes.

One of the key differences between the two organizations is that BXI sells franchises on a geographic basis and ITEX seems to sell as many as are desired. In San Diego County there has just been one BXI office since 1960, while there has been as many as three ITEX offices operating in competition. How does this affect you as a member?

6 ADVANTAGES IN BELONGING TO A FRANCHISE

A. NATIONAL MANAGEMENT TRAINS THE ADMINISTRATORS **33**

"I've been happy with ITEX. I started with them brand new in the business. Some of the ITEX brokers did have existing trade exchanges and just converted them into the ITEX system, whereas in my case, I didn't even know anything about barter. I kind of just fell upon it and started from scratch with no members. I have about 250 members now." David Heller, ITEX, Las Vegas.

B. THE NATIONALLY-MANAGED EXCHANGES ARE MOVING THE INDUSTRY FORWARD

"ITEX has been a very successful company in their marketing plan of expansion throughout the United States, Canada and other countries. It was very significant when they became a publicly-traded company on NASDAQ. That helped open some of the eyes on Wall Street as to what our industry is all about." Scott Whitmer, president, The Exchange; president, IRTA.

C. NATIONAL COMPANIES TEND TO HAVE A SOLID TRADE DOLLAR

"The fact is that ITEX is a publicly-traded company and reports to the Securities and Exchange Commission. What's important about that is that while a lot of barter companies say they run a zero-deficit system, which means that for every dollar of trade credit, there's a matching dollar of trade debit. The only ones that can actually prove that is the ITEX barter system, because they report to the Securities and Exchange Commission, and that's part of our recording. The importance of that to a barter club member is that the trade dollars are liquid, they're spendable. In other words, a broker or even the ITEX corporation can't spend trade dollars that don't exist. We don't create our own currency." Bruce Kamm, ITEX, New York.

D. YOU'RE MORE LIKELY TO GET THE CORRECT 1099s

Although many of the locally-owned exchanges do 1099s and feature quality accounting, you're more likely to get this type of service with the nationally managed exchanges. Mike Baer, the president of ITEX on his corporation's financial responsibility: "We're audited independently annually; we're fully reporting with quarterly and annual statements. It means our life is an open book; we're willing to do that, and we think more people should."

E. LARGER SELECTION OF ITEMS

National exchanges have long promoted that one of their greatest strengths is their ability to offer a much wider assortment of services and products than a single, local exchange. Duncan Banner, BXI, feels his exchange scores well in this category. "Selection is one of our advantages for our customers, which is super important. Significantly more goods and services are available. Even though independently-owned trade organizations can function through national organizations such as IRTA and NATE and make reciprocal relationships with one another, it is nowhere near as convenient as getting in your car, driving up the road, knowing that the check spends three hours from here exactly as it spends here. It's just incredibly convenient. You have more people to earn from, you have more people to spend with, and you have more visibility of who those people are."

Bruce Kamm, ITEX, New York, thinks item selection is an important area. "In a locally-owned barter system, there's limited product and service availability. You'll find that very often a large percentage of the membership is on hold because they have insufficient trade dollars in their account. In a national barter system or a franchise situation—and ITEX is a national barter system not a franchise—what happens is the scope of the product and service availability is much greater, almost unlimited. Of course, you're not going to get the very low margin items, like electronics and computers and appliances and TV's, but the scope of the system is a lot larger. And of course you can spend your trade dollars anywhere in the country.

"For example, an ITEX member in New York City earns his trade dollars, let's say he's an accountant. If he's in a local barter system, he can only spend his trade dollars locally in New York. Whereas, when you're part of a national system, you can spend your trade dollars anywhere in the country, so you can go to vacation in Florida, you can eat in restaurants. If perhaps you wanted a telephone system and we don't have one available in New York, well, there may be one available in Chicago that can be shipped to you. It's just that the scope of trade availability is a lot greater."

F. NATIONAL EXCHANGES OFFER THE CLOSEST WE HAVE **38**
    TO A NATIONAL TRADE DOLLAR

"Probably the most important reason to go with ITEX is we offer universal currency right now that no one else offers, other than BXI, and there's more opportunities for clients to buy and sell nationally and internationally through ITEX than any other organization." Mike Baer, President, ITEX.

3. FULL SERVICE

In theory, a full service barter organization would have several distinct divisions: one for retail trade; another for corporate trade; a third for travel services; and finally a media services section. Often a full service organization also has a store, real estate services, and/or other services, but the first four divisions are the key ones. Each of these sections should be staffed by one or more people who have solid background in the services they are providing.

In theory full service organizations should at a minimum offer those services. Operations like Illinois Trade and Barter Corp. can certainly qualify to be called Full Service. Unfortunately, many retail operations with only a few staff and no real corporate, media, or travel service divisions are calling themselves Full Service operations. As more and more organizations realize the opportunities that offering all these services affords, hopefully we will see hundreds and even thousands of true Full Service operations in the future.

4. START-UP BARTER ORGANIZATIONS

It has been estimated that at least one new barter organization starts up every week somewhere in the United States. As in many other businesses, some of these start-ups will be tomorrow's strong companies, some will always be small and some will fold within months. If you are fortunate to be an early member of a start-up that becomes a major player, their growth can really help your company grow as well. By the same measure, if the barter company folds, you loose all the credits that you have built up in that company.

5. DYING

Every week a barter organization ceases operations somewhere in the U.S. Sometimes they are taken over by another trade exchange and you now have credits with that exchange. In other cases they just plain disappear—and with them whatever inventory of credits you had built up.

The old saying "Any business that is not growing is dying" is especially true of the barter industry. Often a retail barter operation will start with all the right goals and expectations. They quickly get 75 or 100 members. Then they seem to stop growing and evolving. When you're talking with an exchange be sure and check on their growth so that you don't join a stagnate organization. Even larger exchanges go through periods of stagnation—though these tend not to last more than six months or so. Kenneth Meharg, UBE, says, "It's the old adage that you're either going forward or you're going backward—you can't be still."And lastly, in the words of our favorite poet, "He not busy being born, is busy dying." Bob Dylan.

OTHER TYPES OF BARTER

1. CORPORATE

"Corporate trade is the purchase and sale on all trade or part trade/part cash of services or inventories where the barter company is the principal rather than the clearing house." Paul Suplizio, Executive Director of IRTA.

Some retail and full service trade exchanges are now developing corporate barter divisions. But this is really a completely separate rung on the barter ladder. There are over 50 companies that specialize in moving large inventories for various corporations. Sometimes the deals are simple, but more often than not they are involved and intriguing. Other corporate barter companies specialize in the acquisition, transfer, trading and selling of Media. We'll talk more about how these companies work and the importance of media as a commodity in the barter world in chapter 4, *Products & Services.*

Even though most of the corporate trading companies we profile in this book are large corporations moving inventories for other large corporations, Robert Rosenstiel, an independent consultant on corporate trade insists, "Every company of any size needs to understand corporate trade techniques." Mr. Rosenstiel's company, U. S. Intermark, Inc., lists many Fortune 500 companies as clients.

Corporate barter companies and consultants like Mr. Rosenstiel assist corporations in what the corporate barter world calls "asset recovery"—the disposing of assets a corporation would normally take a loss on. The corporate barter company brings a whole new world of contacts and synergy to the table and in most cases will be able to trade that asset or inventory for something that can be used by the original corporation to lower their overhead or conserve their cash flow. It's not uncommon for millions of dollars of, let's say hotel rooms, to be traded for a similar amount of long distance service. The room that would have gone empty is filled and the hotel company's long distance phone bill is taken care of. In other instances a corporation might trade for something they cannot use. For example, let's say a bad deal has been made and a corporation is stuck with media they cannot use. The corporate trader will come in and clean up the deal by moving the originally traded item through their new contacts.

According to Douglas Dagenais, Barter Corp., "Our corporate operation is based on the requirements of the client. In other words, a client has nine dozen of something in an inventory he has to move quickly. It may be difficult to move that kind of inventory through a localized exchange network, and it may be difficult to access things they need through the localized exchange network. Our corporate division, simply due to the structure of the trade agreement, allows the transaction to take place quickly and also adds a new dimension to the purchasing process that fits into large corporations."

Mr. Dagenais continues, "Yes, we have the ability to provide the level of service that any type of client might need and direct him in how he might be best served versus exchanges without a corporate arena might not know how to handle a particular transaction or be capable of handling it, even if they understood it. If somebody came up with ten container loads of a commodity item, let's say grain, it makes it very difficult for a local exchange with 300 clients to know what to do with it, whereas a corporate arena can address that. So we can address every company and provide them the service that meets their needs."

SGD, International is one of the largest corporate trade companies in the world. Its president, Jerry Galuten, reflecting on the size of his staff versus the amount of corporate trading they are involved in, observes, "It's still rather small, because a good deal of everything we do is farmed out. A good deal of fulfillment is farmed out. If it's radio or TV, we got the people that are the biggest in the industry and that buy at the best prices. If it's a major transaction, we'll go in and negotiate ourselves. So the staff is eight, 10 people in this office, a bunch of people in the Orient, several people in Germany. Just throughout the world, we have either agents or people who work for us, but the staff does not have to be big. We get an order from a client for corrugated cartons. We go to one of the leading manufacturers in the U.S., and we place it in his hands. We get an order for a long-distance telephone service from a client, and we turn it over to the phone company we work with and they do all the paperwork; they do all the salesmen's calls and everything else. We just accommodate the bottom line, the final payment. We turned on a company in North Carolina to the tune of about $10,000 a month in phone service. We sent one letter to the phone company saying the bill comes to us against our account and that's all it took. The two letters got set up. I saw tons of paperwork going back and forth between the phone people and the client, but I wasn't involved in it. I only reviewed it. We didn't have to do the work on it. Or consider printing a magazine. We're doing it right now for a client. We set up the printer, and that's all there is to it. We have an expeditor that works for us directly. There's a firm here in New York that has eight or nine people; all they do is expedite our printing work."

Keith Galuten, Jerry's son and also of SGD gives us an idea of the technical knowledge that's sometimes necessary to compete in the world of corporate barter. "I was recently closing a deal with a company that manufactures air shafts. This is a product that is used in the printing industry on printing presses and the plastics industry on blow filament fusion extrusion, or pretty much any industry that requires any type of roller mechanism. This is the shaft that the core goes onto and pneumatically expands and pulls whatever material it is pulling, either paper or plastic. We're providing the company with travel to trade shows, and we're going to be doing quite a bit of printing for them for their manuals and some advertising. We actually solicited this company because we work with many manufacturers of film—plastic film—which is used for duct tape, and we have to work with quite a few home centers that we provide duct tape to. The raw product from duct tape is low density polyethylene with a silver additive. We work with a blow film manufacturer, and basically they tell their plant managers before they make any capital improvements, before they make any purchases, to direct all purchases to SDG. They'll basically give us a list of the large purchases that they'll be making over the year and they'll give us several different manufacturers for each item. We'll just go cold call and solicit new business and put together new contracts."

If that type of deal is a little too technical for you, Keith relates an agreement that was struck with the Queen Elizabeth II—the ship: "We used to provide them with caviar. They are probably one of the largest caviar purchasers in the world. I believe back in the mid-80's, they were using about $1.2 million per year in caviar. We had a deal with a caviar importer. We provided him with packaging and sea freight. He would provide us with caviar on the Cunard Line, which would provide us with cruise accommodations."

Bob Meyers of *Barter News Magazine* puts corporate barter in perspective, "Corporate barter companies do probably seven times dollar-wise the business that the trade exchanges are doing. They're just doing deals on a much bigger scale. They work differently. I guess if you want to be specific they are able to do much bigger deals, because there's a cash component involved. In the trade exchange industry, it's pretty much 100% trade. When you are talking about a supplier, if you will—when you get into big, big numbers—if you're getting a portion of it in cash, it's much easier to digest almost any amount. If you're looking at 100% trade, you have to look at it from a different perspective. You would be amazed at how in any new endeavor things that may be somewhat obvious aren't obvious. You just assume that things are done this way or that way. Well, there is no assumption, especially when you're dealing with an inventory or dollar deals of $1 million, 2, 3, 4, 5 million. It's very black and white if something down the road comes to a head. All of a sudden, you're adversarial with somebody, and you don't have certain things in that contract, you're a dead duck."

Nelson Guyer, San Diego Barter, offers his views on the possible extended benefits of corporate barter: "The biggest benefit of corporate trade is to get rid of excess inventory that's not moving. For that purpose, it's a great market. I see that expanding tremendously. And I see as a flow-over from corporate trade where that will be available to reciprocal retail traders as well. So if an airline wants to sell empty seats in order to get advertising, then those seats would be available to some of the retail reciprocal trade companies to market to their membership. The same thing if a Radisson Hotel does a big media buy and pays for it with rooms, then those rooms are going to matriculate out throughout the system. The exchanges that are well-connected in the industry will pick up some of that trade and make it available to their members on a local basis, even though the transaction was done on a national basis somewhere far from the city where they are living."

2. Media (43)

Only a handful of organizations that focus solely on trading media exist and most of those are in New York, but they are an ever increasingly important player in the national advertising picture. These organizations cater primarily to national corporations and offer almost any kind of media available. We've seen a wide range of media available—national magazines, regional magazines, trade publications, daily newspapers, radio, national television, cable television, and outdoor. Occasionally smaller trade organizations will trade with these operations, but most of their deals are strictly between their corporate clients and their laundry list of media available. For more on media, its availability and how barter exchanges deal with it, see "Media Services" in chapter 4, *Products & Services.*

3. Countertrade (44)

In most instances, when corporate trade is carried out in the international arena it is called Countertrade. In Countertrade the deals seem more elaborate and glamorous and the amounts discussed are sometimes staggering. You can bet when Pepsi-Cola traded syrup to Russia for Stolichnaya Vodka, it wasn't a gallon for a case.

As Bob Meyers of *Barter News* puts it, "International countertrade dwarfs what we're doing here. Enormous amounts of business is done internationally on a counter-traded basis. It's all bilateral, there's no multi-lateral trading at all."

Keith Galuten, S.G.D., gives us an idea of one their international deals: "Dow Chemical brought us in—they manufactured the raw rubber used for the backing of carpeting. Czechoslovakia happens to be a very large manufacturer of carpeting, and they buy a tremendous amount of the rubber. Several years ago Czechoslovakia didn't have the hard currency to pay Dow. Dow did not want to lose the business, so they brought us into the picture, and we found that we could take out product, i.e. carpeting and fluorescent light bulbs and several other products. So what happened was Dow shipped in the rubber and we orchestrated taking out the product from Czechoslovakia, selling it, converting into hard currency, giving Dow back their money plus a percentage of the profit generated, and we kept the balance of the profit. On another deal, we were part of the Yugo America deal, bringing the Yugo cars into the United States. My father was brought in by Armand Hammer into Yugoslavia, because they were selling petroleum into Yugoslavia. There was a restriction on the amount of profit that can be taken out of the country. I believe it was something like 22% of their profit had to be reinvested back into the country. So they had a lot of money caught up, and they had to reinvest it in the country. So Jerry (Galuten) went in and looked at all the different products we could bring out of there, everything from military machinery to consumer products. He met with the head of the wood industry, the automobile industry. Finally it was determined that cars were the quickest and most efficient way to help the petroleum industry get their money out of Yugoslavia. My father was friends with Malcolm Birkland, who used to have the car the Birkland. So my father introduced them to Malcolm, and Malcolm set up the company called Yugo America. They brought in quite a few cars. We were paid for orchestrating the deal—a commission of 2,000 vehicles."

Countertrade is certainly not an area that the average trader gets involved in, but one that you should at least be aware of.

3

BEFORE YOU JOIN

"We always invite people to check us out, to talk to clients, to make sure we have products and services they would want to buy on a trade basis. I would always recommend that someone go in with their eyes open and investigate a little before getting involved in an organization."

Chris Haddawy
Barter Business Network
Reno, Nevada

Tom Archibald, National Commerce Exchange, Tampa Bay, has some advice when considering barter: "One should certainly check out the exchange, and you can do this through the Chamber of Commerce, Better Business Bureau, things of this nature. The International Reciprocal Trade Association has a number you can call. You need to check that out. You need to check out what their goods and services are, is it the kinds of things you might use? Now, I honestly can say that there's very few trade exchanges around that don't have something that everybody needs and uses. We all get up every morning, and we all live a life, and there are many basic things we call come in contact with every day. Many of those things can be traded. So most every exchange is going to have something that one can use. I happen to believe that longevity counts. When I'm doing business with anyone, I like to know they've been doing it for a while. They may want to check these things out, see what you can find out about the owners. So I would expect that one would want to feel comfortable by getting to know a little more, as much as they could, about the exchange. We offer to our potential clients a reference list of clients, business peers, that they can talk to. A few phone calls can certainly be worth a lot. So I highly recommend doing a little research to see what's going on."

32 THINGS TO DO BEFORE JOINING

Since most readers will first join a retail organization, most of the following comments are in that area. Keep in mind the questions you should ask won't vary that much from the other types of organizations.

TALK WITH

1. More Than One Organization

If you are in an area with more than 150,000 people, odds are there is more than one barter organization for you to choose from. Talk with all of them and see which one feels right for you. Remember that most solid businesses that are part of a barter organization are doing between $5,000 and $20,000 a year through the exchange. How much time would you spend investigating a service provider with whom you're going to spend that much each year—one day, two days, more? Plan on spending that same amount of time on this task. Time well spent at the beginning of your barter relationship can save and/or earn you thousands and even tens of thousands of dollars over the upcoming years.

Kenneth Meharg, UBE, reaffirms this approach, "Prospective members need to do their homework. Just like they would do if they were taking on a new vendor or a new supplier, or if your daughter or your son was going off to college. Do your homework, check around, see what's what."

2. THE TOP PERSON

While there are probably several thousand very competent field reps, account executives, and salespeople working for barter organizations within the United States, I've found that it is advisable to ask for the top person and deal with them whenever possible. Only in organizations with more than 20 employees will you find that hard to do. Keep in mind that in most cases the organization or the franchise is owned by the top person. Their income and business is directly related to how many trades are done each month. Astute owners also realize that an organization that isn't growing with good members is dying.

A common statement I've heard made by barter brokers is, "I have several members that would love to use your services (get your products)." Sometimes that has proven to be a true statement and sometimes not. Don't hesitate to state that you'd like to talk to members within the organization. Ask if they have a members breakfast, luncheon, auction, or other type of event coming up that you could attend. The bottom line is that if you don't feel comfortable with the owner/director, then you probably shouldn't join that exchange.

3. LONG TIME MEMBERS

Anyone that has been an active trader for three or four years should have some interesting success stories and possibly some horror stories. What interesting services and products have they gotten. How fairly have they been treated by other exchange members. In good exchanges you will find plenty of people willing to share their thoughts. We found several barter professionals to share theirs:

Don Mardak, Continental Trade Exchange: "If there's a directory, look through it, see who's involved, maybe call a few of those people, get to see if they're satisfied. That's the strongest thing you can do. Get the clients' statements as to what they feel about it."

Chris Haddawy, Barter Business Network: "We always invite people to check us out, to talk to clients, to make sure we have products and services they would want to buy on a trade basis. I would always recommend that someone go in with their eyes open and investigate a little before getting involved in an organization."

Lois Dale, Barter Advantage Inc.: "We keep a Happy Member List. We keep on it a professional lawyer, an accountant, some retail stores, some printers. When a client says, 'Well, can I speak to a client?' we say, sure, make a phone call. Who would you like to pick? Would you like to pick someone in your industry or someone you would buy from? I find once they see that Happy List, they never even call people."

4. SOMEONE IN YOUR INDUSTRY

Ask the top person in the barter organization for the names and phone numbers for several members that are in businesses similar to yours. Then ask how the organization has been for them. Also ask how many businesses they already have like yours. Even though printers are almost always in demand, if the exchange only has 200 members and eight of them are printers, odds are another printer will not get much business. And if you're the fifth plumber in a smaller organization, you won't ever get a phone call.

On referrals UBE's Meharg states, "If you're a printer, I'll give you five referrals from printers; if you're a restaurant, I'll give you six referrals that are restaurants. The bottom is if you can perform the service and service your clients right, that's it in this business, because we don't have anything else to offer except service."

5. VISIT THE BARTER ORGANIZATION'S OFFICES

"It always amazes me how few prospective clients walk into our office and see what the operation actually is. If you're considering a barter organization, walk into the local office, say hello to the people there, and find out on a personal basis: 1) How they are presented—what they are wearing that day? Are they wearing the proper attire to be in a financial business? That is what we are. 2) Do they have an office location? Are they actually operating like a business? People just don't do it. I would certainly do that." Steve White, Cascade Trade Association.

BEFORE YOUR MEETINGS

6. FIND ALL THE LOCAL EXCHANGES

Develop a listing of all the local barter organization. Look in the Yellow Pages under 'Barter & Trade Exchanges'. Call your local Chamber of Commerce. Call IRTA and NATE. Once you've found a few exchanges ask them if they know of any others that exist locally.

7. DEVELOP YOUR WANTS LIST

Before you begin talking with the barter organizations make a list of at least 10 items or services that you would like to get through barter. This is a key tool for successful traders. See pages 71 through 75 later in this chapter for a listing of services that you can typically find through a retail barter organization. Keep in mind that as a new member you are unlikely to get premium items like new computers, four-color printing, airfare, etc.

American Commerce Exchange's Mark Tracy suggests the following questions: "Does the company have a directory? Can you call certain of the members? Are you assigned a trade broker who is going to provide personalized service for you? What are your needs and wants? Look through the directory and see if they can match those needs and wants—not all of them, but the majority of them. Make some phone calls. Find out what kind of members are in the exchange."

8. MAKE SURE YOUR BUSINESS IS STABLE

Don't assume that joining a barter organization is going to solve all your problems if your business has very little cash flow. Once again Cascade's Steve White offers some good advice: "Make sure you have enough money, current cash flow, to join. If you're already having a tough time meeting current obligations, don't join a barter organization, cause it's not going to help you, because whatever products or service you put out will cost you some money. So analyze your own resources. That's the first thing I'd do."

QUESTIONS TO ASK AT THE EXCHANGE

9. ASK SPECIFIC QUESTIONS AND EXPECT SPECIFIC ANSWERS

Enter the meeting with a set of specific questions. This chapter is designed to help you develop those questions. Try to get specific answers rather than generalities. For instance, if you're asking about certain types of members don't put much faith in an answer like 'We're going to be adding a printer (travel agent, whatever) very soon.' Ask for specifics. If this is the deciding element in your joining, you should make it clear that if an acceptable printer, or whatever, isn't available within a mutually agreeable timeline then you get all of your membership fees refunded. This way they have to live up to the promises they are giving you. Also watch out for their salesperson steering you off your set of questions and into their sales pitch.

10. FIND THE FEE STRUCTURES

Not all organizations are created equal when it comes to the subject of fees. Sometimes the salesperson might forget to mention all the following types of fees or they might not be aware of them. Don't hesitate to read the fine print that is normally on the reverse side of the contract. There are four types of fees that you have to keep in mind:

A. Fee to join. This can be as little as nothing or as much as $1,000 or more. Most growing organizations charge between $150 and $400, sometimes with part of that in trade. I've found that the amount charged doesn't necessarily relate to the quality of the organization, but more to how much the owner/director feels they can get at that time.

One of the best ways to see how much they want you as a member is to negotiate on the membership price. If they want you, odds are they will lower the price. If they really need you, they will let you in for almost nothing. Here's the way one broker described his membership fees: "It's $395. Sometimes I'll trade out part of it. If it's a small company, I will take some of that $395 in trade." David Heller, ITEX, Las Vegas.

B. Monthly fees. These are cash and/or trade fees that are collected on a monthly basis by the barter organization. While not all retail organizations have these fees, most certainly do. They range from as little as $10 in trade to as much as $25 cash. Most tend to be around $10 or $15 dollars in both cash and trade and are paid with your monthly statement. Rarely are these fees negotiable.

C. Trading fees. These are the most important fees to any active trader. While they range from less than 10% to as much as 15%, most of the better organizations are at 10% to 12%. For some organizations like Trade Club Exchange the 10% fee is paid in cash at the time that you make the purchase of merchandise or services. For others like BXI, the fee is paid with your monthly statement with the 10% fee occurring when you spend credits. Others like ITEX charge you a fee when you earn credits (6% in the case of ITEX) and a fee when you spend your credits (another 6% for ITEX). Certain barter organizations will allow you to vary these fees if they want you as a member bad enough and they see you as a large enough trader (usually thousands or tens of thousands of dollars in trade volume a month).

D. Annual membership fees. A few barter organizations charge an annual membership fee in cash. If you have been an active trader with them you should be able to get that fee waived or paid in barter credits.

Don't be afraid to bargain on any these points—that's what bartering is all about.

Robert Bechtold, America's Barter Network, Mentone, California, has a different approach to fees: "Our new premier program is unique and geared toward the bigger and more educated barter members. There are no sign-up fees, no transaction fees and no renewal fees. We charge a flat rate of $27 cash and $10 trade per month. Large traders pay slightly different fees."

11. SIZE OF THE EXCHANGE

It takes a client base of roughly 300 active businesses for most exchanges to be truly profitable. Once an exchanges reaches 600 members the range of products offered is probably four times that of an exchange with one or two hundred members. Most of the ones described in this book are well-established and have 600 or more members.

12. WILL THE EXCHANGE BE ABLE TO SELL YOUR PRODUCTS OR SERVICES?

This is one of the key points. If they can't sell your products or services you won't be able to earn any trade credits and the exercise will be a waste. Tom McDowell, NATE: "Part of that due diligence is you need to look at the exchange's membership list and see if there are people there that you could sell to, and then to see if there are people there that you could buy from. That's part of the due diligence that's important, because the idea of trading is to turn over the merchandise and the sales and the revenues so you benefit from it."

13. WHAT NATIONAL TRADE ASSOCIATION THEY BELONG TO

Most quality, well-established retail barter organizations belong to one of the two leading international trade associations. Those groups are:

A. INTERNATIONAL RECIPROCAL TRADE ASSOCIATION (IRTA)

IRTA is the oldest professional barter trade organization, having been formed in 1979. IRTA presently has 177 trade exchanges as members. Annually IRTA holds one major convention (in 1996 it was in Montreal, Canada) and at least one smaller training program on well defined subjects. Headquartered in Alexandria, Virginia, the organization has a ful- time staff of two.

B. National Association of Trade Exchanges (NATE)

NATE may be the younger of the two—having been formed in 1984—but they are no less active than IRTA. NATE presently has 107 trade exchanges as members. Annually NATE holds one major convention (in 1996 it was in Toronto, Canada) and roughly two regional training programs on well defined subjects. Headquartered in Cleveland, the organization has a staff of one.

One of the advantages of belonging to a trade exchange that is a member of IRTA or NATE is that they each have very active ethics committees that review complaints from barter members. Barter Business Exchange's Bob Bagga warns potential barterers, "If you join a barter exchange that doesn't belong to NATE or IRTA, then the barter exchange is not going to be able to benefit from the years of experience from the industry, and they're going to be trying to re-invent the wheel."

Don't hesitate to ask why the barter organization doesn't belong to one of these organizations. If they haven't heard of them then I'd probably do my business elsewhere. For more information on IRTA and NATE see chapter 7.

14. Ask How Prime Items Are Distributed   59

All good exchanges get many excellent items: airfare, computers, wine, and other great items. The process on how those items are distributed will tell you a lot about the exchange. Tom Archibald, National Commerce Exchange, offers some excellent points on his exchange's policy on item distribution: "We have a standard policy here in our exchange. The policy is simple: the upper level management or employees may not have any 'cream of the crop' type trades until it's been offered to clients first. I would fire somebody over that. And here's a prime example. Three weeks ago a client brought in a microwave that was six months old. Beautiful—they only warmed coffee in it. Brought it in and said, "Look, I'll sell it for trade dollars, cause she's got a new one in the kitchen." I'm telling you the truth, as God is my witness, four days prior to that, our microwave at home died. In walks a client with a brand new microwave, and wants trade dollars for it. You want to know how easy it would have been for me to take it home? It would have been easy. The trade brokers were told to sell it, and it was sold that same day to a clients. My wife and I went down to Montgomery Ward that night and bought with our Montgomery Ward charge card, a microwave for the house. You see, the advantage here is that we're going to make considerably more mileage off taking care of our clients than the $175 I had to pay to buy a microwave. Most of the bigger exchanges around the country, all of them feel the same way."

15. How Many Reciprocals They Have

This is very key with independently owned exchanges. Reciprocal trades are how exchanges get items from other exchanges. If the exchange doesn't have any reciprocals or only has one or two it's unlikely that you'll be able to get services outside your area. Most active exchanges that belong to one of the national associations (IRTA and NATE) will have reciprocals with between five and 15 exchanges.

Stan Chaney, Barter Systems, San Antonio, on this subject: "You may want to inquire if you can get advertising for different markets, different states. The exchange that does not have solid communication with a group like NATE is going to limit you in that respect."

16. Find Out About Their Different In-house Services And How They Are Staffed

If you are in a smaller market you shouldn't expect them to have a large staff. Three or four well-trained people can do a wide variety of services for you. The key is do they have staff trained in specific areas that can provide a variety of services to you, the client.

17. How Many Sales Calls Do They Make To Get A New Member?

The better barter organizations—those that can effectively explain the variety of ways that barter can benefit a business—make relatively few sales calls to bring in a new member. Bruce Kamm, ITEX, on his exchange's successful sales approach, "Typically, we have about a 70% closure rate. We're not selling them something they don't want. We're not selling them advertising, we're not selling them water filters. If we can go in and relate properly to a business and go over their business expenses and what they're spending cash on, and how we can eliminate cash expenses with them, or how we can provide alternatives, we've become a business consultant and developed a relationship. Usually it ends in a sale. They open an account and they start trading. I think the only stumbling block is to let business owners know that barter exists. When we go out and talk to them about barter and we teach them how it works, the main thing we get is, 'How come I never heard about this? This sounds incredible.'"

Duncan Banner, BXI, on sales: "We operate entirely on referrals. By the time that we choose to set the appointment and see them, we're signing up more than 50% of the people who we actually choose to go and see or who choose to see us. Half the equation, the 'can you earn business' question, has already been answered. If we're talking to them at all, it means that we have customers for them, and it leaves the remaining question of 'what do we have?' At that point, it's relatively easy to make a fit. So the numbers are very high, you know, a 50/50 chance they'll do it."

18. HOW MANY MEMBERS ARE THEY SIGNING UP A MONTH? 🔵63

This question is, in some ways, more important than how many members they have. The exchange could be new, but if they are signing up 20 to 25 members a month, you've found an exchange with a good future. At the same time, if an exchange has 500 members, but is only adding two or three new members a month then you can assume not much energy is going into the business. "We are growing so fast right now that in our slow months it's more than 40 new members." Bob Bagga, Barter Business Exchange.

19. WHAT RULES ARE THERE ABOUT PART BARTER/ PART CASH TRADES?

Most exchanges have clear cut rules about not allowing part barter and part cash trades below certain minimums—usually between $1,500 and $2,500. If an exchange has no regulations covering this area, it probably means that many of their trades involve cash.

San Diego Barter's Guyer says,"When you charge part cash, you're no longer what's called a 100% trade exchange. That's okay, as long as everybody stays with those rules. Let's say you go to a printer and he charges 50% cash and you're an optometrist. The optometrist says, 'Gee, if I have to pay half cash, I'm going to charge cash.' And he charges 60% cash. Then the restaurant who just got his glasses, who had to pay 60%, says, 'Well, that's a good idea. I'm going to charge 80% cash next time somebody comes in and has a meal with me.' It becomes endemic and chaotic. You're either a trade exchange or you're not a trade exchange, and you have to decide what you're going to do. Our rule is it's 100% trade up to $2,000, negotiable thereafter between the buyer and the seller. And we only charge our transaction fee based on the trade portion, not the cash portion."

Mark Servatius, Allied Barter Corp., Washington, D.C. is adamant about his exchange's rules in this area: "We mandate 100% trade and we expect our clients to trade at fair market value. We do a couple of things to enforce that for our members. One is we get a signed commitment up front that they are going to do it that way. Two is we get feedback via fair trade reports from our clients. We have a form we put out every month that the clients get. We also do 'Mystery Shopping', where a variety of people call up and ask what the rate is and that kind of thing. That has had some interesting results over the last year. Most people honor it. We've been very select about who comes on, and we don't hesitate to throw somebody out if they aren't maintaining their fair trade commitment. Basically, I'm prepared to lose a client any day if it protects the exchange."

20. ARE PRODUCTS AND SERVICES GOING AT (65) FAIR MARKET VALUE?

This is perhaps the touchiest point within the barter industry. You join an exchange and are trading your services at the same price that you would with cash customers and then you need someone else's services and find that they have marked their services up 30% if you are paying in trade.

Susan Williams of Barter Connection has this advice for potential members: "They should think about what the markup is on their product if they are in a product business. They have to know if it makes sense for them."

Jack Schacht, Illinois Trade, remarks on the value of various trade dollars: "Then you have other exchanges who really have a different value on their trade dollar. Their trade dollar is maybe not as hard. That doesn't mean they're bad or they are lesser of an exchange than we are. And I think people are beginning to see this. There are exchanges, for example, that if people want to give us their trade dollars, we want two to one. I think it all has to be ratio, because there's different valuations."

21. ARE THEIR ANY GUARANTEES WITH YOUR   66   MEMBERSHIP?

New exchanges and smaller ones will often provide a guarantee of some sort or another. Some give you trade credits equal to your initial membership fees. Others will provide a package of professional services equal to the fees. Still others will give a one-to three-month trial period to see if barter is for you.

Mark Servatius, Allied Barter Corp., is upfront about his approach to guarantees: "We're also the only exchange in our market that guarantees our start-up fee. We're considered something of a heretic in the industry for doing that. Quite frankly, some of the other owners don't like that I guarantee the start-up fee. I don't want people leaving this exchange somewhere down the road with a black eye. If they leave the exchange, I want it to be an amicable split. I want them to say down the road, 'Well, maybe Allied Barter didn't work so well for me, but it will probably work for you.' So we do quite a bit of work to maintain good relationship with the community."

22. HOW MANY BUSINESSES ARE ON STANDBY?   67

Ask how many of their members are inactive or on standby. This is a good indicator of how strong an exchange is. A business goes on standby when they have more credits than they can find items to spend those credits on. Standby means they are not presently taking additional business from members of the exchange.

Businesses become inactive within an exchange for similar reasons—they are not earning credits or they are not able to find items they want within the exchange.

Lois Dale, Barter Advantage Inc., adds, "Find out how many people are on standby. With weaker exchanges you will have more people inactive than on standby."

23. What Lines of Credit Are Offered?

What types of lines of credit might you expect at the beginning? This is a key question because you normally start off with no ability to purchase other items until you either sell some of your services or are given a line of credit. Once you've seen the typical annual sales volume you will be doing to what level might you have your credit limit raised? If you are a $10,000-to $20,000-a-year trader it is handy to have a credit limit of around $5,000. With larger exchanges I have met people who have had considerably larger credit limits. For traders who average $750 a month or less it is common to have credit limits of between $300 and $2,000.

24. Look For An Attitude Within The Exchange

In your meetings with the exchange staff look for what type attitude they have towards members. Are they treating everyone fairly?

Charles Hernshaw, Coastal Trade Exchange, Inc., Vero Beach, Florida, observes, "Probably the pre-eminent thing would be the tremendous feeling of caring we have about our clients. It's tempting in our business to grab the money and run. We've seen that over the years in barter. There's been horror stories we all know. I think the attitude we have is that we are much like a private bank with private currency and we ought to act like one. It's our members' money and we better manage it well for them. We bend over backwards to give our clients service."

25. How Are Complaints Handled?

Within any business you will have complaints from time to time. Is there a clear cut procedure that treats both sides fairly?

26. WHAT IS THEIR TRADE VOLUME?

Unlike most other businesses, it is not only O.K., but it is appropriate to ask what kind of trade volume an exchange is doing on a monthly or annual basis. Make sure that you are talking about just one side of an exchange, normally sales. Certain exchanges will count both sides in their sales figures and thus double what is their actual business. Typical annual trade volumes for relatively new exchanges would be around a million, for ones with 400 to 600 members, $6,000,000; and for 1,000 to 2,0000 members, $10,000,000 to $20,000,000.

27. HOW IS THE MEMBERSHIP DATABASE KEPT?

While we live in an era where most businesses are using computers, we have seen trade exchanges that are not computerized. Avoid these organizations like the plague since they likely will not be able to adequately service your business. Ask what kind of database program they are using, how often membership directories are updated, how new members are promoted, etc.

28. READ THE CONTRACT

In most cases, trade exchanges are using contracts that were prepared in large part by the nation's more established associations and exchanges. They contain clauses that clearly spell out what is expected of both the member and the exchange, and how each is protected. Some smaller exchanges do their own contracts and they sometimes don't give the protection that you, as a new member, deserves.

QUESTIONS TO ASK EXCHANGE MEMBERS

29. HAS THE EXCHANGE HELPED YOU EARN AND SPEND TRADE?

Both earning and spending your trade is the key to being a successful trader. Duncan Banner, BXI, has the following advice: "Probably the top thing would be to call customers of the exchange and see if they're pleased. You want to get two questions answered up front. Are they going to get business? If you're in some absurd category, the answer may be no. So you want to know what it's going to be like to earn barter. Will there be a great deal of difficulty, as hard as marketing for cash? If the answer is it's going to be as hard as marketing for cash, you might as well go for cash and skip barter. The second thing is what can you get. Not just what can you get today, but what's the big picture in terms of what you can get. Probably the most fundamental role the barter company plays is helping you earn it and helping you spend it. You want to really get into detail with all aspects of how is it going to be earned, how is it going to be spent. Every barter company is different."

30. HOW HAS THE EXCHANGE BEEN ON THEIR PROMISES?

When you are talking with current members ask how successful the exchange has been at producing the items that have been promised. As David Heller, ITEX, Las Vegas, puts it, "I never promise something I can't guarantee I will deliver. I've learned not to promise something in this business based on somebody else's promise to deliver. I will never do that. If I promise something, it's because it's in hand—it's guaranteed. I find too many people in this business tend to tell you they can do something, maybe with good intent, maybe without—some of them are absolute scam artists—but some will do it with good intentions because it was promised to them by somebody else. But there's too many people who will let you down. Just be careful who you're dealing with. Once you deal with somebody who's honorable—I deal on a handshake on a lot of items."

MAKING THE DECISION

31. CHECK WITH THE BETTER BUSINESS BUREAU

Once you've chosen an organization check with the Better Business Bureau to make sure there's not too many complaints against them. Keep in mind that most businesses that have been around for a few years will have one or two complaints against them, but you don't want to go with one that has a laundry list.

You may want to check even further into their organization. NATE's Tom McDowell recommends, "Due diligence. Check out a barter company just like you would anybody you are going to give an open credit line to. Because that's exactly what you're doing. Check Dunn & Bradstreet, check their bank, check their landlord, run a credit report on them, because you're involved in a financial transaction. If you wouldn't loan them money, don't trade with them."

32. WHICH IS BEST FOR YOU: LOCALLY-OWNED OR NATIONALLY-MANAGED

In chapter 2, *What Is Trade*, we discussed some of the key differences between locally-owned and nationally-managed exchanges. This isn't one of the most important deciding points in choosing an exchange, but certainly one that needs to be considered.

33. THE BOTTOM LINE

Once you've met the people in the different exchanges, asked the questions, followed up by talking to their membership and read their materials, you now have to decide which one can do the best job for you. Who seemed most honest? Who seemed most anxious to work with you? Who seemed to have the services you need the most? Who wanted your products or services the most? Once you've answered those questions you're ready to proceed.

FORMULA FOR DECIDING 79
IF BARTER IS FOR YOU

While bartering is definitely not for every business, it should work for more than 70% of all business that exist. Take the following test and work the simple formula to help decide if barter will work for your company:

BUSINESS ATTITUDE QUESTIONS

For each of the following questions give yourself an accurate measurement up to the maximum of points listed after the question. For instance, if you feel comfortable networking with other people, but occasionally feel uncomfortable in those settings, give yourself 4 points.

1. Do you have an entrepreneurial attitude?
   (15 points maximum) _____
2. Do you like to network with other business people?
   (5 points maximum) _____
3. Do you truly want to grow your business?
   (15 points maximum) _____
4. Do you want to have a more comfortable personal life?
   (10 points maximum) _____
5. Do you like to be one of the first to do something new rather than one of the last?
   (5 points maximum) _____

SERVICES OR PRODUCTS OFFERED QUESTIONS

From the sample listing below find your industry or a comparable one. List the number of points that would fit your space within your industry.

1. Retail Sales and Many Services. We are looking for the average mark-up on your products or services. If your mark-up is 40% or greater, 50 points; 30-39%, 40 points; 20-29%, 30 points; 10-19%, 20 points; 9% or less, 0 points. _____

2. Professional Services. If your staff is effectively utilized 79% or less of the time, 50 points; 80-84%, 40 points; 85-89%, 30 points; 90-94%, 20 points; 95%+, 0 points. _____

3. *Manufacturers or wholesalers.* There are two ways to look at this category:
   A. Are excess products or inventory 15%+ of your total inventory, 50 points; 10-14%, 40 points; 5-9%, 30 points; 2-3%, 20 points; and less than 2%, 0 points. _____

   B. Do you have excess products or inventory listed on your financial books in excess of $1,000,000, 50 points; $500,000-$999,999, 40 points; $100,000-$499,999, 30 points; $25,000-$99,999, 20 points; and less than $25,000, 0 points. _____

4. *Media Services.* This is based on unsold media space. If 15%+ of your media space is unsold, 50 points; 10-14%, 40 points; 5-9%, 30 points; 2-3%, 20 points; and less than 2%, 0 points. _____

5. *Hotels.* If your hotel is at 59% or less occupancy, 50 points; 60-69%, 40 points; 70-79%, 30 points; 80-89%, 10 points; 90%+, 0 points. _____

6. *Restaurants.* If your restaurant is at 59% or less capacity, 50 points; 60-69%, 40 points; 70-79%, 30 points; 80-89%, 10 points; 90%+, 0 points. _____

TOTAL POINTS

IF YOUR TOTAL IS: _____

70+ points. What are you waiting for, barter is a natural industry for you.
60-69 points. There's a very good chance that barter would work for you and you should seriously look into it.
50-59% points. Look at the industry again in six months or a year, it could work.
49 or less points. It probably will not work for you.

Let's also look into what your annual trade volume should be in relation to your overall business cash flow. While we have certainly seen successful businesses where barter represents 25% or more of their total cash flow, the norm should probably be less. Bob Bagga, of Barter Business Exchange, observes, "We used to say anywhere between 4% and 10% of total business, but now it's totally open. It should be based on how effectively they can spend their trade dollars. Very simple. If they can spend $1 million in trade, then they should spend that $1 million in trade and sell me $1 million of their product if we're able to buy it."

Lois Dale, Barter Advantage Inc., "I tell people they really shouldn't barter more than 15% of their gross income. It's only an alternative; it's not in place of. Cash is king."

Keep in mind that as the barter industry grows each year, this figure will be increasing.

4

PRODUCTS & SERVICES

"Right now we have members in 500 different categories like printing, radio/TV advertising and restaurants. Now, a printer might also do bindery, so there's two services right there. So in reality we have 2,800 different services within those categories."

Joe Hill
President of Trade Club Exchange
Garden Grove, California

HOW CERTAIN ECONOMIC SECTORS OPERATE IN A BARTER ENVIRONMENT

Barter works well for an amazingly varied lineup of products and services. Items with a 20%+ mark-up are always very successful in any trade exchange. Computers are a very hot item in barter and you can find new computers with all the bells and whistles on them if you are energetic and patient in your search. One item that is always in demand is printing—four color work can be found, but not in every organization, whereas the print shop that can do your letterhead, business cards, and other types of small jobs can almost always be found.

Depending on what part of the country you live in, you might find your exchange stronger with regard to certain products and services than others. You probably won't be surprised to hear that New York City is a strong media bartering center. The midwest is a very strong all-purpose barter center.

Something that is often forgotten in talking about the types of products and services available is that some will only readily be available in markets where they are normally produced. For instance wine that is readily available in the Napa Valley of California where there are dozens of vineyards, is probably not available in North Dakota. Manufactured items often come from the northern Midwest—and thus the exchanges there tend to get more of what is called 'hard goods'. According to Doug Dagenais of Barter Corp., "The midwest has many dimensions. It's industrial; it has a strong retail base; it's sizeable; it does have some destination attractions; it's a center for the home industry and for many national companies. It certainly has more appeal—or rather let's say a different appeal—than San Diego, California. It's different than Orlando. It has such a broad commercial base that it lends itself to having a full-service barter operation, whereas, I'm not so sure San Diego needs a full-service barter operation."

If you operate a print shop with a high cost of hard goods—paper, ink etc.—you're going to approach barter differently from a magazine publisher who brings advertising space to the table or a dentist. Let's take a look at how six sectors of the economy operate in a barter environment.

1. TRAVEL 79

Travel services is one of the fun areas of barter. Just like medical services, it has been estimated that 20-25% of all trading centers around travel. Services available can range from the fanciest hotels in the world to limousine services to get there, to exquisite restaurants, to airlines to get home. We have worked most closely with Mexico, and we have seen nearly every quality hotel trade at one point or another. That would also be true of nearly every country in the world, including the United States.

Why do hotels like to trade? It is very simple—they can never again sell that bed that went empty last night. Aside from a destination like Las Vegas, where hotel occupancies hover around 90% year around, most major business and resort cities have an annual hotel occupancy ratio of between 60% and 70%. That means that on any given night roughly one-third of a hotel's rooms are sitting empty. Their actual cost to trade out that room is very small.

What types of services do hotels get in exchange? The most commonly used service is advertising space in publications, on radio, and on TV. Odds are very good that every day you view or listen to an ad for a travel service of one sort or another that was traded for. And the beauty of barter is that no one knows the difference. Other services that hotels utilize within barter organizations are plumbing, roofing, and cleaning services; telephone systems; and consulting services.

Gary Roberts, ITEX Licensed Broker, Orange County, California, has another perspective: "When I was in hotel management I got a lot of things on trade for the hotel including: resurfacing of the parking lot; a sweeper to come in once a week; the palm trees trimmed; landscaping done; ceramic floors put in all the bathrooms; furniture for the rooms. I was the owner's hero because they wanted to do all these things—but they didn't have any budget for them."

2. Media Services 80

Media is perhaps the most often traded commodity. For purposes of our discussion we are going to include under the category "Media Services" the various functions of the advertising agency and the media provider as well as how you as a potential advertiser should be taking advantage of these services.

Mr. Paul Suplizio, chief executive officer of the International Reciprocal Trade Association (IRTA), has graciously granted permission to use excerpts from his speech "Advertising Agencies and the Barter Business" to the American Association of Advertising Agencies (AAAA) during their Media Conference in Jacksonville, Florida, in 1994. Mr. Suplizio was assisted in the preparation of this speech by Art Wagner of Active Media Services, Scott Thomas of Chicago Barter Corp, and Joe Allen of Joseph J. Allen Communications. Whenever Mr. Suplizio is quoted in this section it is from that speech unless otherwise noted.

The Advertising Agency

To completely fulfill the role of advertising agency your barter exchange would have to offer the following disciplines: Account Supervision, Creative Execution, Media Planning, Media Placement, and Accounting. Not too many exchanges are set up to do all that. In fact, many so called full-service advertising agencies now sub-contract for most of their media placement with companies who do nothing but buy media—television, radio, print, outdoor, etc.

Within a barter environment you will have to do a little extra legwork to take care of your advertising and marketing needs. The ability to find several individual companies to handle these tasks does exist. If you don't find an advertising agency listed in your exchange's directory there are many categories of firms in your exchange—such as marketing consultants, graphic arts or direct marketing—that are set up to handle the creation of your advertisement if you present them with the concept. Creative directors at major advertising agencies are paid low to middle six figure salaries for their ideas, so don't expect a "Where's the Beef" type phenomena for your next campaign. But you should be able to find quality people to assist you with your marketing needs. Since you know your product or service better than anyone else, you need to work closely with whoever you choose to create your ad to come up with something that will get your message across.

THE ADVERTISER

With regards to advertising and marketing, the great thing about barter is that it affords even the smallest operation the opportunity to achieve spectacular results. Barter gives you the ability to expertly market your product and service. Without the ability to tradeout the cost, you probably would never think of attempting a truly professional ad campaign.

If you think you're not ready for prime time as an advertiser, listen to Mr. Suplizio of IRTA: "The majority of the media barter activity remains in the hands of large companies. Major corporations continue to take a leadership role in the acceptance of barter as a method of doing business. That's because they've seen the system work and because holding on to non-performing assets has become such a costly and dangerous option. But increasingly, small and medium-sized businesses are bartering for media through trade exchanges. And this field of barter is growing rapidly."

THE MEDIA

Your barter exchange is often the best place to take your media placement needs. Through their own membership; through reciprocals they might have with other exchanges; or through contacts at major barter media companies, many brokers have the ability to find the right local or national media for you.

With regard to the quality of media now available through barter Mr. Suplizio observes, "In the past, some agencies determined that the best interest of their clients might not be served through a barter transaction. The quality of media being offered through the barter company was deemed inadequate to meet the goals of the client. Some barter companies had limited experience or limited expertise in acquiring the media the clients wanted or expected. Over the past several years, that environment has changed. More and more, the agency community and the barter community have found ways to work together as partners, which translates into greater success for both."

Mr. Suplizio continues, "We have found that media has changed its view of barter and has assisted in our efforts to serve our clients. They have come to see more and more that we create incremental business for them. This is in sharp contrast to the attitude that it's OK for bartered-acquired media to be widely preemptible or made unavailable. As a result, barter transactions can be accomplished using all dayparts, in virtually all markets and in network, spot and syndicated television, cable, radio, outdoor media and consumer and trade magazines. More magazines have begun to treat their ad pages truly as inventory, using barter as a resource to expand their budgets. The ratio of trade credits to cash required for ad space is more favorable now, even in previously restricted publications and in prime dayparts, and has resulted in more favorable spreads for our industry."

3. RESTAURANTS

This is probably the single most popular bartered category. Jack Schacht of Illinois Trade says, "I think restaurants are what I call a natural trade environment. They've always traded, with or without us. They have good leverage. Their meals cost them 30 cents on the dollar, sometimes 25 cents on the dollar. They get new customers. They get to spin off cash customers who come in with trade customers. I think any restaurant that doesn't trade would be derelict. However, not all of them want to join barter exchanges for one reason or another. But I think if we can deliver to a restaurant owner what he wants, why wouldn't he trade? We just go in with that kind of assumption. If we can provide quality exterminating service, carpet cleaning services, duct cleaning services, printing, why wouldn't a restaurant trade? We have 350 restaurants, and I think by the end of the year we'll have 500. We're on a campaign now. We'll maintain about 500 restaurants. We want 10% of our total clients to be restaurants."

Trade Club Exchange's Joe Hill has put a lot of thought and hard work into his True Access plan for handling restaurants in a barter environment. "The True Access plan for restaurants is one item that TCE is doing different than has ever been done before in barter. We are actually going to be on the Internet with TrueAccess.com. What we're doing with True Access is emulating another very successful month-to-month credit card—American Express. With American Express you buy, using their card, and at the end of the month, they send you a statement. If you spent $200 or $500 or $1,000, you send them that much money. Whereas with True Access now, you go ahead and spend month to month, and you send me your gift certificates equal to the amount you were able to spend. If you spent nothing, send me no certificates. It's done on a month to month. Now, we turn around and sell those certificates on your behalf, so the more you spend, the more I'm affected as an advertising company for you, because I will turn up the heat, if you will, and market the heck out of whatever you're doing to sell your certificates. It's working pretty well for the companies who have said, "I've tried barter before. I got too many customers. I couldn't find what I needed. I had 5,000 trade or 10,000 trade credits in my account, and I couldn't get what I needed with it." Well, now, with True Access, if you didn't get what you needed, you didn't give anything to the club, either. So it's pay as you go as you spend with certificates. And we have a very sophisticated little certificate program to track them. In the unlikely event a company goes out of business and we have all those IOUs, so to speak, then we have a way to recall those, because we track where the certificates are going, which is very good, because nothing is worse than going to a restaurant where the certificate isn't honored."

In addition Trade Club Exchange only allows each active member business to purchase a limited amount of any restaurant's certificates each month. This distributes the certificates to a larger number of members, and guarantees the restaurant owner new barter spending patrons each month. These patrons will, thru word-of-mouth advertising, guarantee more barter and cash customers in the future.

Continental Trade Exchange's Mardak also appreciates the importance of restaurants in an exchange's inventory. "In the early days, we used to hoard, ration, our restaurants. I had them issue certificates that said, 'Limited to one certificate per client' or 'per meal', or you couldn't use it on Fridays and Saturdays. Today we have over 60 restaurants. Every one of them is in a deficit, and none of them can get enough trade. They're in a position so we no longer have to ration our restaurants, but we are looking to sell them as fast as we can."

David Wallach, President of the American Trade Association in San Rafael, California, is a firm believer in the overall strength of restaurants in barter. Before a restaurant can join ATA they definitely have to be marketing oriented. "We will not accept a restaurant that doesn't advertise." Mr. Wallach also points out that their current list of restaurants spend $20,000 monthly on advertising that is placed through ATA Media, their in-house media department.

4. REAL ESTATE

If your local exchange doesn't currently have any real estate on trade odds are pretty good that they will in the near future. It is presently one of the hottest growth areas within the barter industry. The following are three different experiences with real estate trades.

Bruce Kamm, ITEX, New York: "We sold a $600,000, 10,000 square-foot warehouse for 100% barter. We sold a condo in Philadelphia on barter. We sold six building lots in the Poconos. We've actually done a barter mortgage for a lot of these properties, where we give the buyer the mortgage in barter, we're the first lien holder on the building or property, and they pay that off on a monthly basis in products and services. The person who bought the six building lots, he's also now trying to accumulate more trade so he can buy some log homes, put those on the building lots, and either rent them out or sell them."

Perhaps the most interesting story about bartering real estate comes from David Heller, ITEX, Las Vegas. "A year ago, I sold a house for a woman from Seattle. She had a house in northern California that sat on 40 acres in a town called Genner-by-the-Sea. It was gorgeous, had a beautiful, unobstructed view of the ocean, on top of a knoll. But the house was built as a pyramid, and it was a hard house to sell. It was built to the scale of the Great Pyramid of Egypt. You could tell how emotionally tied she was to this house. She had it on the market for $495,000, and the best offer she had gotten was $300,000, and the guy was going to level the house—he just wanted the property. She couldn't see herself taking $300,000 from somebody who was going to destroy her temple.

"In talking with her, we determined that she only owed the bank $111,000 on the house. So I found a buyer for her who paid her $125,000 cash and $375,000 ITEX for the house. She was happy, because first of all, she was not living in the house. It was a burden to her. It was an extra mortgage payment, insurance payment, taxes. In her mind she got a half million dollars for her temple. So that was basically a $375,000 trade.

"Now she's buying property in Seattle, she's actually bringing members into the system by finding people for sale-by-owner deals, where they have enough equity. Her first deal she put $40,000 ITEX down on a house, and created a new ITEX member. The woman who took the $40,000 became a new ITEX member to spend it. For the next deal she put down $20,000 or $25,000 on another house. She also bought $17,000 worth of rolling shutters that go outside your house. She's spending her money."

5. BIG TICKET ITEMS

Luxury items come up in trading all the time–and usually they don't last long. This story from Stan Chaney, Barter Systems, San Antonio, illustrates many of the types of things that can be involved: "The latest trade I was instrumental in was a client out of Oklahoma that I hooked up with a client in Austin, Texas. The seller had a variety of merchandise he was trying to move, big ticket items. One was a boat, an 80-foot yacht; another was a $75,000 mobile home, a Jaguar, and a 40-foot yacht. The seller got a return from the buyer of initially $350,000 worth of TV time. There's more to come; we don't know exactly what the balance of the trade will be. The guy that bought the yacht and the bus and the Venture— it's a large cruiser-type of boat—he immediately turned around and traded that."

Tom Archibald, National Commerce Exchange, relates one of his past trades involving similar big ticket items, "My most glamorous trade happened about 13 years ago. Our company was involved substantially in a five-way trade deal for a $1.3 million apartment complex. There were a lot of things involved. I don't have time to explain it all, but basically there was a boat, a large yacht involved, there was a house in North Carolina, a house in Texas, there was a Mercedes Benz. There was a little bit of money in there, and there was some trade dollar credits; the trade bank was the exchange involved in the deal. But the bottom line was, the guy who wanted to sell got stuff that he was satisfied with—between house and boat and barter credit—that he could use for other things, and other people involved got what they wanted to put in their share of what they were doing. Two people wound up as joint owners of the complex, and everybody came out happy in the deal. Of the $1.3 million, there was probably in the neighborhood of about 17% of that was done in cash. People need to realize barter can be done. It may not be always 100% barter deal, it may have to be a little cash in the deal. But the portion that is bartered saves money. It just beats the heck out of writing a check."

Hard goods such as appliances, boats, cars, jewelry and furniture, have their own unique economic set of circumstances that reflect how they are handled by barter exchanges. Except in those cases where you have the opportunity to buy an unsold or out-of-date inventory item, most of the hard goods that you find will be second-hand.

6. NON-PROFITS

Another classification of business that seems to be finding its niche in the barter world is the whole sector of non-profits. BXI's Duncan Banner, is a pioneer in this area and offers his thoughts. "Wouldn't you give more as a business owner if you were giving product or service than you would if you had to write a check? It's really comes down to that. It allows the business owner to be more generous. It allows the business owner to do what they would like to do, which is to help put something back into the community.

"If somebody came to your door asking for a donation you might only be inclined to give them $5, $10 or even very generously $50 or $100. But if they asked for a product they can put into an auction or something that's also going to get your product into circulation and perhaps some recognition of the types of products you offer, that's a fringe benefit, but moreover, your products don't cost you dollar for dollar. They cost you wholesale, you donate them retail.

"So, very simply, it allows people to donate more and to do more. It's an important additional aspect of marketing that sharp non-profit organizations should utilize, because it will help their operation do better by raising more money, even if it's in a funny form—gift certificates or something—there's always a variety of ways to take those things and convert them to things needed for the organization. I have more than a dozen non-profit organizations. Since the information is basically proprietary, I can't say more without their permission. But in general the concept of putting certain items into auctions and then the auctions function as cash fund raisers is widely used. So let's say a non-profit becomes a member of a barter company and they receive donations. They take the donations in barter dollars and they spend the barter dollars on selected items for their auction. Remember, the auction is a cash auction. The auction items turn into cash. Cash goes into the budget. The second way non-profits function is they look for specific budget items that they are going to have to spend cash on, seek that item on a barter basis, and by having that item donated, it's budget relief; it's money they don't have to spend. It represents an immediate cash savings. It's amazingly varied what they do use it for. Literally everything within the organization."

PRODUCTS & SERVICES ⑧⑤
THAT WORK WELL IN BARTER

Carl Buchanan, of Contractor's Mart West, is an experienced trader. His conversation with us points up some interesting facets of the inner workings of the barter business: "I've probably been a member of a dozen trade groups. It seems like you can trade for most anything. I've traded for real estate. I've traded for cars, trucks, cellular phones, fax machines, computers. As a liquidator I purchase products all the time for all cash, and I'm happy to sell at an all trade basis.

"One of the things I've discovered about trading is you can use trade in the cash world sometimes as an incentive to get your foot in the door. I used to work as a painting contractor; it was my first business. I'd go, Hmm, let's see, there's a lot of radio station transmission towers around. None of the local painters seem to do them. They're probably bringing in painters from some other state. Painting contractors bill out their employees for $10 to $50 per hour. The difference is primarily dealing with the skill level and expertise of the painters. If you have a contractor out there doing bottom end maintenance, painting apartments and rentals for $10 or $15 an hour, he needs all that money to pay for gas and basic groceries, etc. The guy who's out there that's a craftsman, is charging $35 or $40 an hour—he can afford to eat in a nice restaurant, he can afford to take a vacation to Mexico. He's going to have more expenses. Therefore, he's the one most likely to be a member. The minimum wage painter is going to join a barter group, but as soon as he realizes that you can't trade for the most basic staples, he's going to tend to filter his way out. So it's not just that all the barter group painters jack your prices up. It's that the painters that are going to be most successful in the barter groups are going to tend to be the more skilled ones. It's a very positive point."

Joe Hill of Trade Club Exchange recently spoke about the variety of products and services he has managed to attract to his exchange. "Right now we have members in 500 different categories like printing, radio/TV advertising and restaurants. Now, a printer might also do bindery, so there's two services right there. So in reality, we have 2,800 different services within those categories."

The following business categories seem to operate quite successfully within the barter arena. Most directories will list these at a minimum while others list everything from soup to nuts. Although we've tried to be very general in this listing, these are pretty indicative of the types of products and services that are available nationwide.

We've used the following coding system to give you an idea of their normal availability:

Almost always available • • •
Occasionally available   • •
Harder to find   •

Accountants • • •
Acupuncture • • •
Advertising:
   Ad Agencies • •
   Media:
      Direct Mail •
      TV • •
      Radio •
      Print •
      Outdoor • •
   Specialties • • •
Air Conditioning/Heating • • •
Air Purification • • •
Aircraft - Charters, Rentals &
      Service •
Alarm Systems • • •
Amusement Parks • •
Animal Training • •
Answering Service • • •
Antiques - Refinishing &
      Sales • • •
Apartment Rental •
Appliances:
   Sales & Service New • •
   Sales & Service Used • • •
Appraisals • • •
Art:
   Dealers • • •
   Framing • • •
   Galleries • •
Artists • • •
Asphalt - Installation &
      Repair • •
Astrologers •
Attorneys • • •
Automotive:
   Air-Conditioning • • •
   Alarms • • •
   Glass • • •
   Leasing •
   Painting & Body Work • • •
   Parts & Supplies •
   Rental • •

Sales New •
Sales Used • •
Service • • •
Storage • • •
Towing • • •
Upholstery • •
Washing, Detailing • • •
Bakery • • •
Beauty Salon • • •
Beauty Schools • • •
Boats - Charters, Sales &
      Service • •
Books, New & Used • • •
Bookkeeping • • •
Bookstores • •
Boutiques • • •
Business Consultants • • •
Carpenters • •
Carpet Installation • • •
Carpet Cleaning • • •
Catering • • •
Cellular Phones • • •
Child Care • • •
Chiropractors • • •
Christmas Trees • •
Clothing, Mens & Womens • •
Clowns • • •
Collection Services •
Computers:
   Consultants • • •
   Programming • • •
   Rental • •
   Sales New •
   Sales Used • • •
   Service • •
   Software • •
   Supplies • •
   Training • • •
Construction • • •
Contractors • • •
Copiers:
   Rental • •
   Repair, Sales & Service • • •

Supplies • •
Copy Service • • •
Cosmetics • • •
Costume Rental • • •
Counseling • • •
Credit Information & Repair • • •
Dating Service • •
Delicatessen • • •
Dental, Lab & Supplies • •
Dentists • • •
Dermatoligists • •
Desktop Publishing •
Draperies • •
Dry Cleaning • •
Drywall • •
Electricians •
Electrolysis • •
Electronic Equipment &
       Supplies • •
Employment Services • •
Equipment Leasing • •
Estate Planning • •
Eye Glasses/Contact Lenses •
Fax Machines:
    Repairs • • •
    Sales & Service • •
Financial Consultants • • •
Fire:
    Alarm • • •
    Extinguishers • • •
    Sprinklers • •
Flooring • • •
Florists • • •
Formal Wear • • •
Furniture • •
Garden & Lawn Equipment • •
Gardeners & Lawn Service • • •
Genealogy • •
Glass, Sales & Installation • •
Graphic Designers • • •
Guns • •
Hair:
    Barbers • • •
    Products • • •
    Removal • •
    Replacement • •

Handyman • • •
Health:
    Clubs • • •
    Food • • •
    Products • • •
Hearing Aids • • •
Hotels & Motels • • •
Hypnosis • • •
Immigration Service • • •
Insurance • •
Interior Decorating • •
Investigators • •
Investments • •
Janitorial Service & Supplies • • •
Jewelers • • •
Laminating • • •
Leather Goods • • •
Limousine Service • • •
Locksmith • • •
Magazine Subscription
       Services • • •
Mailing, Lists & Services • • •
Martial Arts • • •
Masonry • • •
Massage • • •
Mini-Storage • • •
Mobile Homes • • •
Mortuaries • •
Motorcycles • • •
Moving & Storage • • •
Nail Salons • • •
Nightclubs • •
Notary Public • • •
Nursery • • •
Nutritionist • • •
Office Equipment & Supplies • •
Optometrists • • •
Orthodontists • • •
Pagers & Paging Service • • •
Painting • • •
Paper Products • • •
Party:
    Decorations • • •
    Planning • •
Para-Legal Aid • • •
Pawn Shop • • •

Payroll Service ••
Pest Control •••
Pets:
   Boarding •••
   Grooming •••
   Sales & Supplies ••
Pharmacy •••
Photo Processing •••
Photography •••
Physical Therapy •••
Plumbing •••
Physicians ••
Plastic Surgeons •••
Printing:
   Basic Printing •
   4 Color Printing ••
   Color Separations ••
   Pre-press Services •
   Supplies ••
Public Relations •••
Real Estate, Rentals & Sales ••
Resorts •••
Restaurants •••
Resume Service •••
Rolfing •••
Roofing •••
Safes •••
Sailing •••
Sales Training •••
Satellite Antennas ••
Schools •••
Secretarial Services •••
Shoes ••
Signs •••
Skin Care •••
Skylights ••
Spas & Hot Tubs •
Sportfishing ••
Sporting Goods ••
Steam Cleaning Services •••
Stereo Equipment ••
Swimming Pool:
   Maintenance •••
   Repair ••

Supplies ••
Tile ••
Tailors ••
Tanning Salons •••
Tax Services •••
Telemarketing •••
Telephone:
   Answering Service •••
   Cellular •••
   Long Distance Phone Cards •••
Systems •••
Television, Sales & Service •••
Termite & Pest Control •••
Tickets •••
Toys •••
Trade Shows •••
Travel:
   Airline Tickets •
   Hotels/Motels •••
   Travel Agents ••
   Timeshares •••
Tree Trimming •••
Trophies •••
Tropical Fish ••
Trucking ••
Tutoring •••
Typesetting •••
Upholstery ••
Vacuum Cleaners, Sales &
   Service ••
Veterinarian •••
Video Equipment, Sales &
   Service ••
Vitamins •••
Wedding Services ••
Weight Loss •••
Welding •••
Windows:
   Cleaning •••
   Screens ••
   Shades ••
   Tinting ••
   Replacement & Repair ••
Wine ••

If you constantly refer to your trade club's directory, you'll soon get into the habit of "thinking barter first." We recently moved the corporate offices of our publishing company. The first thing we did was consult the trade directories of the local exchanges that we deal with on a regular basis. We ended up using five separate service providers, all within the barter industry, that made the entire move a lot easier to take, financially. Using the category list above, here's who we worked with:

1. *Movers.* The professional moving and storage company we hired for our move included everything—trucks, moving equipment and labor—on trade. Among other things, the owner of the moving company uses a considerable amount of his trade dollars in local restaurants buying lunches for his work crews.

2. *Alarm System.* The building we were moving to already had an alarm system in place but it needed activation. It was a simple matter to look at the directories to see a selection of five alarm companies to choose from. A quick price and service capability comparison later and our system was on and being monitored—all on barter. Any one of these companies could have installed the entire system on trade as well.

3. *Telephone System Installation.* We have a fairly extensive telephone system involving six separate lines, computer networking, as well as dedicated modem and fax lines. We own the equipment and can operate it, but removal and installation is obviously best left up to professionals. Once again the entire job was done 100% on trade.

4. *Janitorial Service & Supplies.* It's amazing how much of a mess you can make moving 40 file cabinets and assorted desks, book cases and computer equipment around. There were several full service janitorial companies available to us, but we choose to use a very professional cleaning woman who makes extra barter dollars after hours doing general house and office cleaning.

5. *Catering.* We held an Open House shortly after settling in that was completely catered by two trade exchange members: a local deli and a Mexican restaurant. We had no complaints about the quality or quantity of food.

5

ONCE YOU HAVE JOINED

"I think a good trade exchange will watch and analyze a client's buying habits. I know we watch very carefully what percentage they spend on personal and business-related products. We talk to them about their overall amount of trade they're doing. If we see someone starting to build a balance who has been pretty much of a buyer/seller client, we'll call them up and see if their buying habits are changing, if they're downsizing, if they're doing something different."

Tom McDowell
President
National Association of Trade Exchanges

4 Goals For Your First Year Of Trading

1. Find Your Learning Curve

We all learn at different speeds and the new traders among you will be learning from many different trade exchanges. It is safe to say there is no magical timeline for learning how to be a successful trader.

Douglas Dagenais, Barter Corp. observes, "No matter what the level of investigation, there's a learning curve for any company for how they are going to handle barter and incorporate it into their operation, so do a little at a time. A little may be a different number for every size company, but do it gradually. Make sure they know in fact who their product is going to be sold to and whether it's accomplishing what they want to do in terms of the sales, so they turn the transaction as quickly as a cash transaction."

Timothy Ritchie, Merchant Trade Inc., says, "Everyone should be open to considering barter as a part of their lifestyle. They should also realize that barter is not the same as cash, that cash will get you things you can't get with barter, and sometimes it takes patience and understanding in order to effectively use the barter system."

2. Update Your Wants Lists

During the phase of finding an exchange you should have developed a wants list. Now that you've joined an exchange you need to look at that list again and see if it is still valid.

3. Develop A Barter Budget

The first task is to estimate how much you'd like to spend on barter this first year. This goes hand in hand with your wants list. What percentage do you want to use for direct business expenses; for staff bonuses or even as part of their salary; and finally, for your personal enjoyment. Once you have developed your barter expense budget then you need to see how you will earn it. This is the time to start putting your broker to work—ask them to review your plans and ultimately make sure that they are working to both help you get your products and services sold and to get you the things you want to purchase.

4. Meet With Your Broker

This is the time to start putting your broker to work—ask them to review your wants lists and barter budget. You need to make it clear that you are expecting them to produce some results for your business, maybe not in a week or two, but certainly within a six-to eight-week period. Ultimately make sure that the broker is working to both help you get your products and services sold and to get you the things you want to purchase.

13 THINGS A BARTER BROKER CAN DO FOR YOU

Barter exchanges are in the service industry. Your broker exists to serve you. Here's how Steve White, of Cascade Trade, sums up what he does for his clients: "Several things. For one, they're all assigned a broker. The broker's income is directly related to what's generated by their client. So they have a major interest in making sure that person gets business, because when they get business, they're going to go ahead and spend that credit. We publish a directory. We publish it annually; we update it monthly. All new clients go in the monthly update. We do a monthly newsletter; new clients are again put into that. They're allowed to put flyers into the newsletter. We do a weekly hot list on Wednesdays where we list about a half dozen items, so if they had something that was a hot item, we could put it in there. Every weekend, we do another hot list called *The Trader*. It's more of a classified, a little more extensive, maybe 50 items." That's a lot of good service.

Chris Haddawy, of Barter Business Network explains that the member also has some responsibilities to work with the broker. "What I always teach our clients is you're going to get as much out of it as you put into it. If we have a mixer and you don't show up, that mixer did you no good. If you come to the mixer and you bring marketing materials and you bring business cards and hand them out, you will get additional business. When we put a directory out, if you place an ad in that directory, you will get additional business. If you pick up the phone and call and introduce yourself to other people in the network, you will get more business than if you don't. So if someone wants to work the system, they'll get a lot of business. If they want to sit around and wait for the system to work for them, they'll get some business, but not nearly as much as if they worked the system. And we give them all sorts of ways to work the system."

Let's take a further look at what services most exchanges are offering their clients.

1. MEMBERSHIP DIRECTORY

This is the single most important piece of marketing that your broker is going to do for you. Almost all retail barter organizations put out a directory. Most directories are issued annually or quarterly and updated monthly, so it's important for you to get your listings correct from the start. We say listings because you should try and cross-reference your business as much as possible. Think of ALL the services your company has to offer and see how many category headings there are for what you do. If you run a beauty salon that also sells beauty supplies make sure you're under both listings. Your goal should be to make it as easy as possible for your potential customers to find you.

Duncan Banner, of BXI in San Diego, is a strong supporter of publishing a directory. "You can't always take the time to entirely rely on a broker so if a barter company doesn't have a directory, don't join. It has to have a published directory. You don't want somebody entirely deciding for you who you get to see and who you get to do business with. You absolutely want to have that kind of flexibility. The directory is real important. How often is it updated? Quarterly, monthly? Any less frequently than that and it's probably out of date. It's no good, it's useless, it's wasted time."

Use your membership directory like a phone book and just as regularly. Refer to it when you need a product or service and advertise in it if possible. More often than not this is the first place your fellow members will find out about you. So keep your listings up to date and as descriptive as the amount of space allows.

2. MAILINGS

Ask your exchange if you can include your own flyer in their next mailing to the membership either as they send out the new directory or when they do any special mailing. Some might charge you a small mailing fee, but most we know of do it on a regular basis at no extra cost. It's your responsibility to supply as many flyers as there are members to the exchange on their deadline. You'll never find a more cost-effective way of doing a direct mail effort.

If you have a product or service that you wish to market outside your immediate area and you belong to an exchange with branch or franchise offices in different cities, you may be able to include your brochure or a flyer in a corporate mailing the headquarters do from time to time to all of their various offices. Basically you now have a secondary sales force wherever your club's got an office. Even if you're not able to piggy back on a corporate mailing it should be possible to get a mailing list of the branch offices and do your own direct mail piece just to let everyone know you are a member and are open to business from their area.

3. NEWSLETTERS

Most of the better barter exchanges send out a newsletter to keep their members up to date on, among other things: current events in the barter world; changes in the exchange; new members; a list of what people "Have" to trade accompanied by a list of what people "Want" to get on trade; specialty items that have just become available; and possibly a list of restaurant and hotel script that you may purchase directly from the exchange with your barter credits. Usually these newsletters are sent out weekly or, as is more often the case, monthly. It's an excellent way for the exchange to stay in touch with its membership.

4. MIXERS/NETWORKING

We attend a variety of luncheons and dinners hosted by trade exchanges where a great deal of very important networking occurs. Meeting your fellow members over a good meal with the chance to give a brief "commercial" on your business is basic personal public relations and one of the very best chances you'll have for marketing your product or service.

Mike Hoffman, area director, BXI South Florida, is a believer in the regularly scheduled mixer: "Thirty to 100 people attend our monthly trade evening dinners. It's free to members. Restaurants fight to host it."

As Barter Connection's Susan Williams, puts it, "We do business with people we like, the people we know. We'll do business with them first. So the more people you know within the exchange, the more customers you'll get." Adds Williams, "We have probably a half dozen mixers a year spaced out in different ways. We have a very large holiday affair that works very well for us. We do probably a week's worth of business in four hours at a holiday affair. We also have a small traders' emporium where traders can come to the office and buy things there."

Steve White of Cascade Trade also offers regularly scheduled events. "We do an event every month, the second Thursday. We call them Info-Mixers. The first hour is dedicated to representing the barter program to new clients. But it's also set up so that old clients can come in and get re-educated on it, or they can send in their general manager or their maitre'd or whoever runs the show, send them in to get a reintroduction. The second hour is devoted to just a general mixer—champagne, beer, wine, it's catered and all that stuff. Last night we had one, and there were 15 clients–15 companies—and they brought somebody, so maybe there were 20. We do a seasonal thing also, a holiday auction in November and we have about 250 people at that. It's just a big party, but they are very, very good."

5. Weekly Faxes

A good barter exchange has to communicate with its members on a variety of levels. The periodic—usually weekly—updating fax is one of the best tools a broker has to expediently reach the entire membership. If your club doesn't currently offer this feature, encourage them to do so. The fax can be as simple as a listing of new members who have signed up that week, a list of new items that are available and a reminder of important upcoming meetings.

6. Club Store-Showroom

Charles Hernshaw, of Coastal Trade Exchange, is fairly typical of brokers who also operate a retail shopping outlet for their members. "We have a showroom that is not terribly large. It's probably less than 400 square feet, equipped much like you would expect a store to look like. We have back wall jewelry cases, we have gondolas like you'd use in Wal-Mart. In fact, we bought them from Wal-Mart when they moved to a new location. We have a little bit of a lot of things. It's an ever-changing vista. And I kind of laugh when I say that, cause we never know what's going to come in tomorrow. Much of what we have in the showroom is on consignment from our members. Some we directly buy from the members and put in here to sell. Much of it is from other exchanges we reciprocate with. And we even from time to time buy things for cash and put them in the store on trade, just to keep our members happy. Right now we have a lot of Easter merchandise. In fact, I was just told we're getting low on bunnies. We've got no more in the warehouse, so we're going to run out of bunnies; we'll be out by late today. We try to get things in with a seasonal approach to it. It has proven very popular with our members. It's a lot of extra work. It doesn't generate that much money, of course, because we're working on the service charge. We pretty much sell it for what we buy it for. Once in a while, we find a very good deal, and we can mark it up a little bit on trade, but most of the time, that's not true. But the members just love it. At Christmas, of course, it was a madhouse. We had members double-parking outside to run in for one more thing. It was kind of fun to watch."

Continental Trade Exchange also offers a retail outlet for their members. Don Mardak says, "Go to our office. We also have a showroom in our office, so we encourage people to come in and visit us. Many times people like to come in for the restaurant scrip to buy it right at the office, because there's so much else to shop for. Our showroom has about $300,000 worth of products. We have about eight jewelers in our program, and some of them would prefer to not have clients coming into their showrooms. They'd rather have them come to us, and we buy the jewelry from the jeweler, take a discount on it, and we sell it to our clients in our retail showroom."

7. SCRIPT 96

Issuing script is an excellent marketing tool many barter exchanges utilize. Some members—for example, restaurants—would rather not deal with the time and nuisance involved in accepting a barter check for each transaction, especially if that transaction is in the $5 or $10 dollar range. Other companies want to keep a limit on the total amount of barter they do in a given period, so they will issue script—or allow the broker to issue script—only up to that predetermined amount. They will either get their trade credits up front or as the script is redeemed.

Script can also be an attractive, colorful piece of advertising material that your broker will use to promote you. We see a lot of script changing hands at mixers and other networking events. It's fun to watch the sharks circle when a certain pizza restaurant's script becomes available. Done right, script can be a powerful point of purchase sales piece.

8. Auctions

A barter auction offers an exciting opportunity to purchase—often at deeply discounted prices—various items that you don't see everyday in either the membership directory or on the fax line or in the newsletters. Many members hold back some very high quality items just for the yearly auction that many barter exchanges hold. Members liquidating estates often show up at these auctions with household good including furniture and appliances. Great discounts on office equipment can also be found. If you enjoy the action of an auction, you'll especially enjoy one where you get a chance at some great deals while spending your barter dollars. A word of warning. Don't get so involved in the bidding process that you lose your common sense when it comes to pricing. A lot of members new to the barter world have a tendency to look upon their accumulated barter account as "play money" and spend it unwisely. Remember the hard work you put into creating, marketing and selling your products or services and put as much "smart shopper" sense into your barter purchases as your cash ones.

9. Fax Back

With new technology comes better quality service. Exchanges can now offer information to their members via a fax-back system. It's a good way to get the latest information on availability of goods and services. Like many other exchanges, Jack Schacht of Illinois Trade offers this service. "We have what we call an electronic directory, which is a fax back service allowing clients to punch in a product and service code and then get complete listings of who the vendors are within those product and service categories."

This type of system is particularly useful within large, multiple office franchise operations. It really helps your business trip planning when you can get a list of hotels and restaurants in a particular city that are members of your exchange. Of course the system is only as useful as the amount of time and dedication the operator puts into keeping it up to date.

10. Keep An Eye On Your Spending Habits

When you're a new member of a barter exchange, one of the more important things your broker can do for you is to make sure you are spending within your limits. As Tom McDowell of NATE explains, "I think a good trade exchange will watch and analyze a client's buying habits. I know we watch very carefully what percentage they spend on personal and business-related products. We talk to them about the overall amount of trade they're doing. If we see someone starting to build a balance who has been pretty much of a buyer/seller client, we'll call them up and see if their buying habits are changing, if they're downsizing, if they're doing something different."

11. SPECIAL EVENTS

The most common special event is usually a trade fair put on annually and often held during the Christmas season to attract the holiday barter shopper. Exchange club members are invited to take booth space to show off their wares in a convention center, hall or warehouse rented for the occasion. We've been to some fairly large "trade fairs" with row after row of exhibitors selling everything from luggage, travel accommodations, jewelry and new age vitamins, to chiropractic care, tailored suits and Christmas trees. Many traders wait until just such an event to do the majority of their yearly trading or to bring out their exclusive, expensive items such as Rolex watches, fur coats and Italian shoes.

Event planning is a very important part of Scott Whitmer's overall marketing plans. As president of The Exchange he's interested in providing as much service as possible to his members. "We've very involved with our clients as far as events. We do two auctions a year. We do *Trading After Hours* similar to chamber meetings on a regular basis at our restaurants. We sponsor different non-profit organizations, such as the theaters, operas, ballets in town, and do fund raising and different events for them. During the holidays, we have pies and cakes for Thanksgiving; we have Christmas trees on our lot for the holidays. Then just about every month we do a different event for our clients; we have at least 10 a year. We just did a *Trading After Hours* last month that attracted over 350 of our clients for an evening. During our Baseball Night that we have with the Orlando Cubs, we have a big picnic beforehand. Last year we fed over 1,100 clients at that event, and this year's already tracking to be much larger. It's the most successful event I've heard of in the country. We have all-you-can-eat hotdogs and hamburgers and all the fixings, and we have a big picnic from 4:30 to 7:00 before the baseball game. We rent out the entire park and give away the tickets to our clients. So it's a very successful event for us. We pride ourselves on our events and our interaction with our clients. We get to know them better, we get to know their concerns. If they have any problems, we can address them quicker. When our clients get to meet and shake hands and say hello to one another, they tend to do more business. And, it's a tremendous promotion for the exchange, it really is. It works out very well."

A great example of doing the "out of the ordinary" or "special event" to promote barter and provide extra service to the client is the work that Nelson Guyer of San Diego Barter is doing in the southern California area. "I do a Barter U on a regular basis at the Advertising Arts College here in San Diego, a workshop telling small businesses how to tap into barter and trade up to 10 or 15% of their business. If they don't do that, they're leaving money on the table. There's tremendous interest on the part of micro and small businesses towards tapping into what I call a secondary profit center—barter. We encourage non-members to attend our Barter U, we encourage every small business or potential small business to take a look at barter as a secondary profit center. Never to replace your primary center. In fact, if you don't have a primary profit center, you should defer getting into barter."

Lisa Peters of Trade Systems Interchange offers her members an ongoing, special event she calls *Barter Mania*. "It's a game. A lot of people say we hold contests. We just call it a game. They can win prizes, earn points for doing specific things, such as referring someone who becomes a client. They get extra points if that's a targeted member, such as a restaurant or printer. They get extra points if the referral calls us instead of us calling them, because they've gotten so excited. They can get points for displaying their TSI sticker at their place of business or their car, for coming to a luncheon or a mixer. There's other ways of earning points, and there are levels and prizes. The object of the game for us, from our perspective, is to get them a little excited, get them motivated, let them have some fun, and be thinking about TSI so we get some referrals for new members, but also so they might do a little more volume. Something a little different, a little fun, unusual, out of the ordinary. People get tired of doing the same old thing. The goal of the game is to become the *Barter Maniac* and win the big prize."

12. On Line Service

Nothing has so excited the barter world nor opened the potential for bartering on a national and international basis to the general public as the capability to access the availability of barter goods via the computer. Some exchanges are now experimenting with listing their members and making their various goods and services accessible to other members of the exchange via a computer and modem. Excellent values on goods and services are waiting to be found with this method.

However, the most exciting prospect for on-line barter lies in the advent of the World Wide Web. Scott Whitmer, president of The Exchange and also the current president of the International Reciprocal Trade Association (IRTA) says his organization is exploring the possibilities. "IRTA has contracted with a company to come out on the Internet. That's all in progress. We've already got commitments from over 50 companies to go on line day one, and that's in the very near future. We'll have an IRTA directory, because it's IRTA-sponsored. Any member of IRTA can come on line and have their own web page. So we'll have a directory of all the IRTA members, and the ones who choose to go on line will have their own web page and listing service for availabilities of hotels, excess inventories, advertising, things of that nature. We won't be listing products. We're hoping to attract major retailers who will recognize the barter industry as a way to liquidate and to move through excess inventories."

ITEX is another company that has pioneered electronic barter transactions. Mike Baer, the president of ITEX says, "I think we also offer state-of-the-art Internet and on-line barter technology for our clients. Our competitor doesn't offer that. Now that the computer generation is of age, people aren't afraid to log on to their home computer and dial into the Net. They're able to be their own trade broker with us. So it makes it a lot easier for them to find what they're looking for and sell what they have. For our brokers as a business opportunity, it makes wonderful sense to link up with us. Because, again, our technology is second to none. Our brokers spend their time enrolling clients and helping those clients trade. All the transactional posting is done electronically through our point-of-sale swipe box, which is just like running a VISA card through a little point-of-sale terminal. We have our own proprietary system there. So it's easy for our barter clients to trade. We remove the paperwork, which is a big load off our brokers' backs and allows them to spend their time making money putting trades together."

13. Credit Extension

Normally, most barter organizations will extend an initial line of credit to new members to get them up and bartering as soon as possible. Your initial credit line is usually just enough to get you by until your first sales. Periodically you may need to request an extension of your line of credit for a special purchase. Your ability to get that extension most likely will be based on your trading history. If you spend an average of $5,000 a month within the barter system your broker will take that into consideration when determining your new credit line. Your ability to generate a certain level of sales over the course of a year also weighs heavily in the exchange's decision.

Just because you're now dealing in a barter economy don't expect the rules of loan evaluation to be any less stringent. Depending on the philosophy of your broker, getting a barter loan can be harder than a cash loan at a bank. Some brokers and exchanges believe in a free economy where fairly large lines of credit are given routinely, while others' beliefs are 180 degrees in the opposite direction.

NATE's Tom McDowell, has strong views on the subject. "I think one of the problems too many trade exchanges have is they extend credit on trade without using the same decision making process they would use if they were loaning cash. That's the reason a lot of trade exchanges have inflated systems and their members are not receiving value—because they're not treating the trade like money. One of the things NATE has worked on for years is to try to create a mentality with the exchange owner that it is money; it does purchase quality goods and services; that you can use it to acquire the same things you can acquire with cash, so treat it that way. I think credit lines should be on an individual basis. They should be based on credit-worthiness and the ability to repay within the barter system, not just arbitrarily given because they give you a credit card to pay their fees."

David Heller, the ITEX broker in Las Vegas, basically agrees. "I got one client an $11,000 credit line because he needed to purchase his liability insurance through me and the premium was that high. It was an air conditioning contractor that I knew we would have enough business for to justify that. I couldn't authorize it on my own. As an ITEX broker we have to go to the corporate office for anything that large—anything over $1,000 now. As long as they know there's a reasonable expectation of getting paid, they will authorize."

If this is an important area of concern, you should discuss the exchange's credit philosophy at length with your broker before joining.

5 WAYS TO GET MORE TRADES

1. TELL YOUR BROKER WHAT YOU NEED

Ask almost any barter broker what they tell their members when asked how to get more trades and most likely the first thing they'll say is "I tell them to call me." You'll hear versions of this refrain from all sizes and types of trade clubs, companies and exchanges in every part of the country. The direct lines of communication between the members and their trade broker is the key to successful trading. As Art Goehring of the Columbus, Ohio, based Tradecorp puts it, "If they call us, we'll assume it's an order, and we'll try to fill it any way we can."

Keep a list of the things you have not been able to find on trade and periodically give it to your trade broker as your "wants" list. If you are ready to spend your barter dollars on a consistent basis for those items, your broker will do her/his best to sign up a company that can provide them.

Joella Smith, a trade broker for San Diego Barter, attests to the hard work brokers put in on behalf of their clients. "So far we're probably well over 80% in being able to meet the needs of our members. The ones we haven't met so far we're working on, because they're usually very large items. We have a request for a hot tub. We have requests for things as large as vacation homes and real estate loans. So we're pretty wide-spread, and so far we're doing quite well in meeting the needs."

2. TELL YOUR BROKER WHAT YOU HAVE

Think of your trade exchange and all its trade brokers as your secondary sales force. One of the principal rules in selling anything is "know your product." You wouldn't send an in-house, salaried, salesperson out to sell your product or service without some fairly extensive sales training. So get to know your trade brokers and make sure they have a good idea of exactly what your company is all about. Do a sales presentation for the brokers at the exchange or take one of them on your next sales call. The more they know about you the better they'll be able to represent you to the other members of the exchange.

3. Be Creative

The more you know about the barter industry the better equipped you're going to be to make that special trade that might take a little extra thought. Maybe you might have to throw a little something extra into the mix to get a particular item that's normally difficult to find on trade. You'll want to make sure you don't trade yourself into a deal that would have been better done strictly on a cash basis.

Byron Lester of MerchanTrade Inc., in Waco, Texas, likes to see a creative type enter the barter world. Observes Mr. Lester, "Someone who is good with numbers, and will devote the time and energy to eagerly work the system on a monthly basis, is an excellent candidate to be a consistently successful trader over the long haul."

4. Learn About Your Fellow Members

There are a lot of barter club members out there that expect deals to come to them and will not go the extra step that's sometimes necessary to make a deal work. By learning as much as you can about your fellow members, you'll be in a much better position to make a lot more of your own deals work. The more trading partners you have that are active and happy the better off the whole exchange is going to be.

5. Be a Barter Ambassador

Let's face it. There are always going to be personal and business expenses that you won't be able to find within the barter industry no matter how hard you try. We contract for a considerable amount of printing in the course of a year and a great deal is done on barter. If we get a bid from a cash printer that's in the neighborhood of our barter bids we'll mention that we already have a competitive bid and it's all on trade. Of course we then add, "It's a growing industry. Maybe you should look into it." In a year or two, who knows, that printer just may be trading with you. The more you talk up the advantages you've found in barter, the more likely you will be able to fulfill more of your barter needs in the future.

TAX IMPLICATIONS ⬤108

The tax consequences of trade is certainly a key area. As accountant Anne Adams of Palomar Tax Service, who has been an active barter trader since 1993 and member of several exchanges, notes, "I tell clients that bartering units are exactly like a dollar of cash and that the value of the barter credits should be included in income in the year the units were credited to their account. I tell them that when they file their tax return, they should lift out the 1099 they received from the barter broker as a separate schedule and attach it to the return to show they included it. Even if they don't get a 1099, they should include it as income anyway."

The barter professionals we consulted were eager to add their thoughts on the important subject of taxes.

Scott Whitmer, The Exchange & IRTA: "There is not any real tax advantage to trade. The advantages are the new business that you receive, the cash that you conserve by using the trade that you earned to offset normal cash expenses. So the tax issue, I think, was very important for the industry."

Don Mardak, Continental Trade Exchange: "Some possible barter members state 'If you're going to tax me, I'm not going to do it.' The proper exchange response should be, 'Well, you surely wouldn't want me to encourage you to be part of something that's a tax scam or tax evasion, would you?' This helps make barter a totally legitimate above board industry. It's not part of the underground economy. And it is that way because of the TEFRA Act."

One key item with barter is to make sure you keep good records of your barter income and expenditures—just like you do with regular income and expenditures. Anne Adams, Palomar Tax Service: "When a business sets up their books, they can set up a barter account that works exactly like a checking account. On a monthly basis, keep up with the income and expenses from the barter just the same as they would with a checking account. Also if they paid personal expenses by barter dollars that they earned as a business savings, take it against the drawing of the dividends from the company some other way. They couldn't call those personal expenses a business expense. I reconcile my barter statements when they come in, and include it as income and include it as cash barter unit, then delete it Barter units paid out."

The accounting industry in FASB 93-11 recognizes trade dollars and credits in accounting doctrine.

Anne Adams, Palomar Tax Service: "As long as the IRS doesn't get upset because people are bartering under the table and not being up front and not claiming it, which has been a problem in the past. In fact, that's why I never wanted to be involved in barter. But now with the advent of the clubs where 1099s are issued and it's recognized by the IRS as being an up-front, above-board type of thing, I think as long as it's not abused, it will continue to grow."

Concludes Ms Adams: "I think barter is a wonderful concept. When ITEX, came into San Marcos, I saw a write-up in the *Blade Citizen*, and I immediately went over because I was intrigued by the concept. I think for existing businesses that already have a cash clientele and aren't living from paycheck to paycheck, that it can be an excellent way to increase business and to get certain things done that you want without having to spend cash. Services we've gotten include roofing work, construction, printing, and other things that a business needs, because we own the building."

8 THINGS TO DO YEARLY

1. DECIDE IF YOU BELONG TO TOO MANY OR TOO FEW ORGANIZATIONS

If you're doing an average of $500 a month in barter and you belong to only one exchange you are probably missing a chance to make barter work even more effectively for you. Remember that all exchanges are not created equal and that if you can find a way to spend $6,000 a year in one exchange the odds are good that you'll spend another $6,000 a year within another quality exchange. Remember to once again go through many of the steps that we outlined in chapter 3, *Before You Join*.

2. DEVELOP A NEW WANT LISTS

Give some thorough thought for ways that barter can help reduce your cash expenses at the office, at home, and even with your employees. Don't be afraid to make this list 20 or 30 items. And remember that every year your business and personal expenses can change.

3. MEET WITH YOUR BROKERS

Your should meet with your trade brokers far more than once a year, so if you haven't seen them in a year, set up a meeting. Keep in mind that they're only human and they sell best the accounts that keep in contact with them. This annual meeting can also serve as a time to go over your wants lists and reemphasize the items that you have.

4. DECIDE WHAT BUSINESSES YOU CURRENTLY PAY CASH THAT YOU WOULD LIKE TO HAVE ON TRADE

If you're not—as we discussed earlier—a *Barter Ambassador*, you're missing one of the best ways to save cash. This approach works best once you've had some solid trade experiences and can share them with other businesses.

Now when a business phones us trying to sell their services we ask what trade exchanges they belong to. Often the salesperson will ask for some information so we fax them a very basic page on trading. This has lead to more than a few businesses joining an exchange. We got a beautiful office with an ocean view on a sublease this way. Another time we found a major four-color printer. More often we will get someone into trading that fixes equipment or has office supplies.

If your company deals with 20 companies or suppliers on a regular basis it would be a workable annual goal to work toward getting two to three of them to join a barter association.

An additional feature of this program is that many trade exchanges pay a bonus to members who bring in new members. Some of the exchanges even pay those bonuses in cash. Continental Trade Exchange's Don Mardak: "Members need to keep us aware of their needs. If you have a supplier you're dealing with that you'd like us to try to enroll, let us know that. We continually push them to provide leads for us. We do pay them for the leads in trade $50 to $100, depending on the quality of the lead."

5. DEVELOP A NEW BARTER BUDGET

At least once a year you need to review your barter budget. Do you now want to spend more on your basic expenses. Perhaps you should reward some hardworking employees with a nice trip, or do you want to fix up or add expansions to your house.

Nelson Guyer, San Diego Barter: "Your expenditures need to be commensurate with the new business that you bring in. Otherwise, it's not working, because your final acid test whether the trade dollar is replacing a cash dollar in expenditures is when it's used, when it's spent."

In a normal business atmosphere we would like to have as many sales as possible. When you're dealing in barter it is wise to set clearly defined goals and stick with them until you know the correct level of barter for your organization.

Lisa Peters, Trade Systems Interchange: "They should analyze how much barter they can do in their business. The conventional wisdom is that probably no more than 10% of annual sales."

6. KEEP HUNTING FOR WAYS TO REDUCE YOUR CASH OUTFLOW

One of the best suggestions that we've heard was to offer to pay your outstanding debts with barter. Susan Williams of Barter Connection adds, "Barter has even been used for child support and alimony payments. Payments are used for dental, health, etc."

7. DEVELOP A GOAL FOR EACH BARTER ORGANIZATION YOU BELONG TO

Make a list of goals and desired trades for each organization you belong to, taking into consideration the strengths and weaknesses of each association. Our trade per association ranges from as little as $2,000 to $3,000 to as much as $60,000 per year.

8. WHEN YOU HAVE PROBLEMS

Occasionally, as with any industry, barter club members will have a problem of one sort or another with their exchange. What should they do? The first thing is re-read your contract. Many contracts state how complaints will be handled. Another avenue is to contact IRTA and/or NATE.

Scott Whitmer, The Exchange and IRTA: "The IRTA ethics commit-tee hears numerous cases throughout the course of the year. Some are from trade companies dealing with other trade companies, and a number of these situations are clients and members of the exchanges that have a problem with the exchange. We do very thorough research on any of these complaints. Our ethics commit-tee does an excellent job. In most instances, once we get involved, the problems are resolved. Just by the fact finding and encourag-ing both sides, we sort of help mediate the situation. As a result, there's usually very positive results from this process."

6

THE FUTURE

"It's like we've barely scratched the surface of things that can be accomplished with barter."

Rachel Taylor
Barter System Inc.
San Antonio, Texas

16 VIEWS ON BARTER'S FUTURE

1. OVERALL (117)

None of us has a crystal ball, but it's safe to say that barter is going to grow dramatically in the near future. Within our lifetime we should see the Department of Commerce issuing monthly reports on the status of barter and its effect on our nation's economy.

Susan Williams of Barter Connection proclaims: "The growth is going to be explosive. As more and more people realize the benefits and what they can do with it, whether it's large corporations moving inventory that may be discontinued into markets where they currently don't have any product at all, or whether it's smaller companies that have more of a local market, I think more companies will discover this tool for their business and be enthusiastic about it."

Barter System's Rachel Taylor says: "It's like we've barely scratched the surface of things that can be accomplished with barter."

2. THE CORPORATE AND RETAIL TRADING WORLDS (118) WILL FORM CLOSER TIES

Until recently there has been a distinct line between the retail trade exchanges and the corporate ones. Some did deals together, but not on a regular basis. Now many of the larger retail exchanges have added a corporate division. Here are three industry insiders views:

Harold Rice, American Exchange Network: "Linking the corporate trades to the retail trades. The retail trades are the logical outlet and the final resting place for all these computers from the corporate world. It makes sense to link those more frequently and more efficiently so products can go from the manufacturer right to the retail trade person. And the corporate traders and the retail trade exchanges, instead of operating in two separate worlds, can mesh."

Bill Jeffery, Barter Business Exchange, Coquitlam, B.C. Canada: "I see us trading truckloads of commodities. Dealing more with the manufacturing end. That's my expertise because I'm already in with the manufacturers. Getting out of the retail level trades and going more commercial."

Mike Baer, president, ITEX: "Corporate barter will continue to flourish. Large corporations, national and international, with surplus inventory or any manufacturing overruns will look to barter as a way to move surpluses and trade for the things they need, to help everything from preserving their balance sheet to looking for a good return on their investment and offsetting a lot of their legitimate cash expenses."

3. NEW PLAYERS IN THE INDUSTRY

Major business powerhouses are presently analyzing the barter industry to decide what, if any, role they should play in it. Here are two well respected traders thoughts on the subject.

Lois Dale, president, Barter Advantage Inc., New York: "I see barter being much more global in effect. Three months ago American Express contacted me, because they were thinking about going into the barter business. They were thinking about doing all the actual transactions for the barter industry. I thought it would be the coolest thing that could happen to us. They were thinking of either buying up the firms or just doing the transactions."

Alan Zimmelman of BXI West Los Angeles: "I was interviewed by someone who consults to Mitsubishi who stated that Mitsubishi was interested in getting into the barter business—but they found BXI to be too small."

4. ELECTRONIC COMMERCE

It's old news now that the Internet is changing many industries and barter is certainly one of them. As of May, 1996, over 50 barter companies have a presence of some sort on the Internet. Every month, five or more trade companies are establishing their foothold on this important vehicle for exchanging information. Here are some of the traders thoughts:

Bruce Kamm, ITEX, New York: "Electronic trading and the fact of connecting broker offices in various cities kind of makes the United States smaller and makes the trade dollar easier to spend by use of electronic mail and the Internet."

Scott Whitmer, president, The Exchange; president, IRTA: "The next most significant aspect of the business is communications with the Internet. IRTA right now has contracted with a company to go on line within the next 30 days to be able to offer products and inventories on a world-wide basis on the Internet. I think that's going to be very, very significant."

Bob Meyers, *Barter News*: "On our web site we get 150 to 200 hits a week. I think the Internet is a prototype of what is going to be fantastic someday. If they adopt a currency that all of the exchanges will use with one another and the information and availabilities are on the Internet, I suppose that could be a factor for having exchanges have a lot more goods and services available, because they could access it through this common currency and the Internet."

Mike Neal, VP Marketing, ITEX: "Take all the glamour and glitter out of the Internet, and what it really does is a couple of things. One, it puts clients in touch with clients. A client can look on there and try to find all the florists in New York, and they'll just get a list of it.   Many trade exchanges, I think, are a little closed-lipped about their client list for whatever reasons. We don't cater to that philosophy. We have our client list right out there. If you get on *Barter Wire*, you can look at any client we have in the entire exchange. And that's really important, because our job again as brokers is to put the deal together. Second, there's a system called Haves & Wants which is a data base organizer, where clients can put up what they have for sale out there, their wares and their goods for sale, and other clients will be able to search through that list at Haves & Wants and find it and do matches. I think we've got just over 4,000 regular users on it, which is a good percentage of our clients obviously."

5. YOU'LL BE ABLE TO SET UP A COLLEGE TRUST FUND 121

In the near future you will see many private colleges in the United States signing up to trade within barter networks. Why, you might ask? Because their overhead on one additional person in a class is very low. At the same time colleges, like many other businesses, are short on funds. Ray Bastarache, president, Barter Network has just signed up two colleges. For Sacred Heart College, his alma mater, he supplied a company that did a $25,000 public relations campaign. Bastarache states: "That campaign made them believers."

6. A COMMON BARTER CURRENCY 122

The concept of a common barter currency that can be used within any exchange has been promoted for more than a decade. The major benefit of such a system is that it would allow for far more reciprocals than now exist. The major problem with the concept is that, unlike the U.S. dollar, not all barter currencies are created equally.

Among those who like the chances for a common currency are:

Mike Baer, president, ITEX: "Our goal for the longest time has been to promote some sort of unification, so we don't have what we have right now—500 separate barter companies and 500 separate currencies. We believe the ITEX trade dollar will be one of those standard currencies. We think there should be more. We support the development of an alternative currency for use in our industry through IRTA. It's basically a private money, and we believe that the backing of most trade currencies, particularly ITEX's, is stronger than the U.S. dollar. The U.S. dollar is backed by a federal reserve note; we don't really know what that really means. But we do know that trade dollars are backed by the pledges of the assets of our membership. At ITEX we have some other things backing the trade dollar. We like to see universal currency and a universal clearinghouse. We don't think ITEX will be the only gainer. We do think there needs to be three or four major players with universal currencies."

Chris Haddawy, Barter Business Network: "The people who have barter exchanges around the country really need to work together more for a common currency. It won't be that way unless people come together."

Bob Meyers, *Barter News*: "I think a common currency will come about within the next year through IRTA. It's conceivable that NATE will have theirs, because there's still situations where both organizations would more or less want their own controls. I think that's a plus. Will you see one coming together where 100% of the industry would work? I don't see that happening for the foreseeable future."

Mike Neal, VP Marketing, ITEX: "I think a common currency is going to happen, regardless of whether ITEX is the one that brings it to reality or not. We hope that we are in the position to be able to work well with other trade exchanges to make that dream a reality. A client has the right to spend a trade dollar once they've earned it."

Steve White, Cascade Trade: "I'm spending a lot of my time working towards a common currency."

Scott Whitmer, The Exchange; IRTA: "In the future we're looking as an industry at a very important aspect of a common currency, and that's being investigated, to enable the reciprocals to trade much easier. I think the Internet and the common currency will truly open a global barter market."

Alan Zimmelman of BXI West Los Angeles: "I think that a common currency is an idea that will launch our industry into the stratosphere and have a major effect on the business industry. The difficulty with it is that it has to be monitored and that it has never been done before so it has to begin slowly. I see it happening within a year and another year to perfect it. It's a two year program."

Then there are those who say it will never happen:

Duncan Banner, BXI: "No chance, because I think that at that point it would gain the attention of the powers that be and they wouldn't stand for it. That currency might be considered a security and have to be regulated. But I don't think there's any possibility of there being a second currency in the economy with anywhere near the numbers of U.S. currency in terms of just the volume. Maybe one barter company will evolve and it will become somehow a clearinghouse in the same way that a few banks clear almost all the credit card transactions. That role may be taken on by the big financial institutions, the same people who clear credit card transactions."

Jack Schacht, Illinois Trade: "You're never going to have the whole industry working together with common currency. I don't see how that could ever be done. I think that's one of barter's pipe dreams. I think you can find exchanges who can work together with a common currency. For example, I work with 12 exchanges who we feel are the strongest exchanges around the country. We open up our systems to each other pretty wide. That is a common currency.

As we go to press, IRTA has set up a special task force empowered to create guidelines for a common currency.

7. Barter Companies Going Public

This is presently one of the hottest items of discussion within the barter industry. Presently only one exchange, ITEX, has gone public. IRTA's Scott Whitmer: "ITEX was one of the pioneers in this area, and I think it's very significant for the industry. I applaud ITEX's efforts. They've done extremely well. I look for more barter companies going public in the future. I've heard of a number of them going through the process as we speak, so it's just a matter of time."

Mike Baer, president, ITEX: "We certainly hope that happens, because we've been out there pounding the drums with NASDAQ to make them aware of what's going on in our industry and let them get a feel for it. We think that what we have done will make it easier for others. There should be more publicly traded barter companies. What the industry needs is more cash, more capital infusion for growth and expansion. It's been a real cash-starved industry. There's tons of good operators out there, but we need to see some consolidation, number one, and number two, we need to see more publicly-traded companies who can go out and raise capital, develop this whole commerce concept. So we're not only in support of that—we would assist some of these companies in doing that."

8. ITHICA HOURS - ANOTHER VIEW ON HOW BARTER MIGHT WORK IN THE FUTURE

As you may have gathered from the book thus far, there are many different approaches to the barter industry. A very grass roots program has been developed by Paul Glover, a community economist with a background in city management, in Ithaca, New York. The program has generated over 1,000 participants since it started in 1991 and has generated inquiries from cities across the United States.

Here's Paul Glover's description of how their program works: "Here in Ithaca, New York, we've begun to gain control of the social and environmental effects of commerce by issuing our own local paper money. Thousands of purchases and many new friendships have been made with this cash, and about $1,500,000 of local trading has been added to the Grassroots National Product. We printed our own money because we watched Federal dollars come to town, shake a few hands, then leave to buy rain forest lumber and fight wars. Ithaca's HOURS, by contrast, stay in our region to help us hire each other. While dollars make us increasingly dependent on multinational corporations and bankers, HOURS reinforce community trading and expand commerce which is more accountable to our concern for ecology and social justice. Here's how it works: the Ithaca HOUR is Ithaca's $10.00 bill, because ten dollars per hour is the average of wages/salaries in Tompkins County, New York. These HOUR notes, in five denominations, buy plumbing, carpentry, electrical work, roofing, nursing, chiropractic, child care, car and bike repair, food, eyeglasses, firewood, gifts, and thousands of other goods and services. Our credit union accepts them for mortgage and loan fees. People pay rent with HOURS. The best restaurants in town take them, as do movie theaters, bowling alleys, two large locally-owned grocery stores, many garage sales, forty farmer's market vendors, and 250 other businesses.

"Hundreds more have earned and spent HOURS who are not on the Ithaca Money list. Ithaca's new HOURly minimum wage lifts the lowest paid up without knocking down higher wages. For example, several of Ithaca's organic farmers are paying the highest common farm labor wages in the world: $10.00 of spending power per HOUR. These farmers benefit by the HOUR's loyalty to local agriculture. On the other hand, dentists, massage therapists and lawyers charging more than the $10.00 average per hour are permitted to collect several HOURS hourly. But we hear increasingly of professional services provided for our equitable wage.

"Once issued, anyone may use it, whether signed up or not. Ithaca Money's 1,300 listings, rivaling the Yellow Pages, are a portrait of our community's capability, bringing into the marketplace time and skills not employed by the conventional market. Residents are proud of income gained by doing work they enjoy. We encounter each other as fellow Ithacans, rather than as winners and losers scrambling for dollars. The Success Stories of 300 participants published so far testify to the acts of generosity and community that our system prompts. We're making a community while making a living. As we discover new ways to provide for each other, we replace dependence on imports. Yet our greater self-reliance, rather than isolating Ithaca, gives us more potential to reach outward with ecological export industry. We can capitalize new businesses with loans of our own cash. HOUR loans are made without interest charges. We regard Ithaca's HOURS as real money, backed by real people, real time, real skills and tools. Professor Lewis Solomon of George Washington University has written a book titled *Rethinking Our Centralized Monetary System: the Case for Local Currency* (Praeger, 1996) which is an extensive case law study of the legality of local currency. Dollars, by contrast, are funny money, backed no longer by gold or silver but by less than nothing—$5 trillion of national debt. Local currency is a lot of fun, and it's legal. HOURS are taxable income when traded for professional goods or services.

"To give other communities a boost, we've been providing a Hometown Money Starter Kit. We've sent the Kit to over 400 communities in 47 states so far. To get one, send $25.00 (or 2.5 HOURS) or $35 U.S. from abroad, to Ithaca Money, Box 6578, Ithaca, NY. 14851."

Mr. Glover concludes, "Thirty cities across the U.S., including Santa Fe, NM; Madison WI; Hardwick, VT; Waldo, ME; Bethleham, PA; five systems in Canada and one in Mexico are in the process of starting a program similar to Ithaca HOURS."

9. MAJOR INTERNATIONAL GROWTH

Outside the U.S. barter will grow in two different ways: countertrade between countries and the growth of retail and corporate trade exchanges. As you will see in the next section, the United Nations is entering into the countertrade industry in an effort to help developing countries. Countertrade has become an major force for many former communist countries as the mode of exchange with more developed economies.

In the last five years we have seen rapid growth of retail exchanges in other countries. Canada has a number of very successful exchanges. The exchanges that have developed in Australia have also found businesses willing to participate. In the United States right now retail and corporate barter exchanges work with approximately one percent of the U.S. businesses. The country with perhaps the best market coverage is Iceland where 470 out of the island's 11,000 businesses are part of Nordic Barter. The means that Nordic Barter has captured 4.3% of the county's businesses in it's short three years of existence.

Kenneth Meharg, Unlimited Business Exchange: "I think you'll see more barter being done in other countries that will filter back to us, just like what we discussed now with Atwood Richards and other big corporate buyers. It's changing every day; our business is changing every day."

John Attridge, director, The Queensland Trade Exchange, Bundall,

Australia, reflects on barter's international growth potential: "International trade will grow enormously. While many countries do not have hard currencies, they do have inventories. There will be government incentives to improve the balance of trade–tax incentives and export incentives. Companies will also look internationally to expand their markets."

10. THE UNITED NATIONS - HELPING COUNTRIES DEVELOP THEIR ECONOMIES

In March 1996, Jerry Galuten, president of SGD International out of Riverdale, New York, was appointed as a special senior consultant to the United Nations Development Group.Dr. Bendek is the director of that division. According to Mr. Galuten: "The post will be dealing with countertrade for smaller and developing countries. The U.N. figures it's opening doors to countries that have goods and services, and that want to trade those for things they need. They don't have hard currency.

"As an example, one of the former Soviet countries came in to see me last week. They produce oil, but they can't sell the oil very easily because they're in the middle of the continent and they don't have access to water for shipping. The problem is the Russians don't want to give them time on the pipeline because the Russians sell their own oil. They're sort of blackmailing them or holding back on giving them time. So what we're doing is—and the refineries are working at about one-third capacity right now and there are three refineries—we are contracting to supply equipment so they can make what's called naphtha, and from the naphtha we're going to put in equipment so they can make polymer[?] and from that small investment for equipment to make polymer, which are plastics. So we're making the finished products, so to speak, and don't have to transport the crude oil. We transport a finished product. They'll get paid in the equipment initially to do this, and then they'll be free to sell the plastic on the open market throughout the world. We'll have first right of refusal because we'll foot the bill for the equipment to start with.

"We have the same thing with a mining operation where they don't have the capitol, but they have the copper ore. We'll arrange trading the copper off to a major copper buyer. In exchange they will finance the initial equipment from proven resources.

"We have another one. China needs urea, which is a fertilizer. Again, back to Russia. Russia has stopped the feed stock of the natural gas to the plant that is no longer in Russia—it is in another country, which was formerly part of Russia. So they are operating at 10% capacity. They owe Russia x number of dollars. Russia doesn't want to ship them any more feed stock, any more raw materials, to make the urea. So we're able to get a commitment from China to buy the product, and we're using outside money to pay off the Russian government and turn the line of credit or purchase the feed stock again and get the factory working. We have a ready customer and a ready supplier to get that thing rolling.

"We also have people in China right now. We have people all over the world that work for us, with us, both agents and employees. The U.N. transaction opened a lot of doors for us. It gives us reliability, it gives us presence, it gives us an acknowledgement by a world organization that, hey, we're here, we do it. We're not fly-by-night."

Adds Keith Galuten, S.G.D. International Corp., New York City, "We're getting involved with supplying goods to the United Nations. They were going out and paying hard currency for product that they need. We're saying, 'Don't pay in hard currency, pay in product.' Governments that are members of the United Nations contribute product, then we have the ability to help them move that product. The appointment to the U.N. was a very big step for the company; it's going to bring in a lot of interesting and profitable deals."

11. THE INDUSTRY WILL WORK CLOSER

While associations like NATE and IRTA have helped development, the industry needs to find a way to better promote itself. That should happen in the near future. As Stephen R. Covey stated in the widely respected book, *The 7 Habits of Highly Effective People*, "Interdependence is a higher value than independence."

Alan Zimmelman of BXI West Los Angeles, agrees, "Barter is needed. I would like to see the barter companies work together to share. Mr. Terry Neal, the founder of ITEX, recently said a very wise thing, 'A rising tide raises all ships.' If everyone worked together we can make all businesses aware of the industry. It will take some effort, but it will be worth it. What if we could say that we had a million members in total—and we went to VISA and asked them to oversee our transactions. Then we all could focus on what we do best—helping trades happen."

12. A True Public Relations Effort For The Industry Is Needed

Like many industries in their infancy, barter hasn't taken the time on a consistent basis to go out and toot it's own horn. All the people involved in the industry devote their energies into growing their own exchanges. Within two years I'm confident that we will see a major, united public relations effort on behalf of the industry. It certainly is needed.

The following is a short story from Continental Trade Exchange's Don Mardak that shows how most of the media reacts to the barter industry: "It seems when certain people hear about this who have not heard about it before, they respond in such a positive way. We did a few press releases a few years ago just to announce we had moved from my house into an office. We didn't say it was my house. We just said, 'Continental Trade Exchange has expanded and is moving to a new office,' and sent out a press release. Some papers, at least four of them, came back to us and asked to do an article on our company, because they thought it sounded so unique and so special. So we got free publicity. When we hire new employees—when we bought the trade exchange in Green Bay—we issued a press release, and we got other newspapers asking to do an article on us."

13. Creating A National Barter Day - A Proposal

We recommend to the barter industry—IRTA, NATE, and anyone else interested—that we get together and work towards a National Barter Day. We have days, weeks, and even months honoring thousands of different causes, organizations, and types of people. The main purpose for these days is awareness. Barter needs a national awareness day.

Activities could include events held by all the exchanges across the country; a meeting of industry leaders with the President or Secretary of Commerce; and, in time, a network television special on the barter industry.

During such a day, aside from the normal proclamations given both locally and nationally, articles detailing the benefits of barter would appear both locally and nationally. Industry leaders would run a series of ads promoting the progress that barter has made and list a number of phone numbers that those interested could phone. We see these full page ads running in the *New York Times, Los Angeles Times, USA Today, Wall Street Journal, Business Week, Forbes,* and on and on. Of course, many of these ads would be run on trade.

Showing a united industry front would go a long ways towards bringing in new businesses. Individually, members of both the NATE and IRTA Boards of Directors have expressed an interest in the project. Shall we all, together, take the next step?

14. BARTER IN THE YEAR 2000

It has been estimated that presently one percent of the businesses in the U.S. are actively involved in barter at the retail, corporate, or countertrade levels. In the future it is safe to say we will see substantial growth—but how much? The following are the thoughts of different exchanges on the percentage of business that will be involved in barter in the year 2000.

Paul Suplizio, IRTA: "We see the number of businesses bartering through barter companies growing from 400,000 now to 1.6 million in a decade. That would be a penetration of 25% of the small businesses with more than one employee."

Duncan Banner, BXI, San Diego: "It seems like the industry is doubling every couple of years."

Douglas Dagenais, Barter Corp., Oakbrook Terrace, Illinois: "Certainly it's more a norm today than 15 years ago. People are aware of it; it's more of a normal business practice. Technology and the evolution of exchanges, their size, their sophistication, their successes with clients, is going to make it more of a normal business practice. Some things like hula hoops become hot overnight. I've been waiting for barter to become hot overnight for 15 years. It's a business tool—it's a business practice. It's something you have to work at every day, and five years goes pretty quick."

Lois Dale, Barter Advantage Inc., New York: "I just know we're in a growth pattern. People will still only barter a certain percentage of their business."

Nelson Guyer, San Diego Barter: "I see barter as becoming a major player in sustaining the great American dream. It gives us the advantage that big business has always had but never publicized, because trade is going on in the Fortune 500 companies in a major way."

Chris Haddawy, Barter Business Network: "At least 10%. Just makes too much sense."

David Heller, ITEX, Las Vegas: "I understand it's about 15% in Europe now. I can't see why we can't reach that eventually. In fact, I do have a recip with Eastern Europe's largest trade exchange. They have offices in 12 cities."

Charles Hernshaw Coastal Trade Exchange, Inc.: "I see it developing very rapidly. As I say, we're three years old and we feel like an old-timer now, because we meet so many people that are in it six months or less. I see it gelling into a formalized niche business where people will have heard of it. I suspect we'll see regulation along the way. Our association tells us it will probably be the SEC that does it. As I mentioned, we've had some problems here in the Florida area with trade exchanges that have been less than savory in the past. If it would keep those kinds of people out of our business that's probably good."

Joe Hill, Trade Club Exchange: "If history has proven once again to repeat itself, barter will continue to grow, because in the past barter has seen very nice growth. I see it growing annually 20%, 25%, even faster than that, as the acceptance continues to grow."

Bill Jeffery, Barter Business Exchange: "Probably 4% to 5%."

Bruce Kamm, ITEX: "I see the growth being tremendous. We've seen New York easily grow 100% every year over the last three years."

Tom McDowell, NATE: "Maybe 1.25%, 1.5%. The opportunity isn't going to be presented to that many people. We're limited as to how many trade exchanges there are out there. So by the sheer numbers, when you really look at it based on how many businesses there are and how many barter salespeople there are to present the opportunity, if we can climb in five years to 1.25%, 1.5% of the market share, we've done an excellent job."

Mike Neal, ITEX: "ITEX will probably have 250, maybe 300 offices. But beyond that, you will have seen us develop strategic alliances with a number of good, strong exchanges. We are allowing these strategic alliances to come in, whereas at one time we had to have the contractual rights of the client, and we had to buy the client base. We are now expanding our philosophy so that we're going to be able to perform accounting services. Our clients are going to be intermingled so that they can exchange currencies. That way there's a certain amount of autonomy and independence on the owner/operator exchange. And what we're really good at is accounting. The things that keep them doing it are independence, autonomy. They have the entrepreneurial bug in them and they want to maintain that."

Lisa Peters, Trade Systems Interchange: "We have made a lot of progress in the exposure for the barter industry—positive exposure—developing stature, respect, integrity. You could see a huge explosion in the market penetration, simply because our time is here."

Timothy Ritchie, Merchant Trade Inc.: "I think we'll be somewhere at 5% to 10%."

Jack Schacht, Illinois Trade: "I think probably our experience is pretty much a reflecting of the whole industry. Now that we've been around 12 years, we grow on the low end 15% a year, on the high end 25% a year. I suppose if you multiply that out by the exchanges around the country, I imagine their growth is comparable, so I would hope that in the next five years as an industry, we'll double."

Mark Servatius, Allied Barter Corp.: "I see probably three to four times as many trade exchanges opening up and probably a large consolidation movement with the franchises. The watchword in the industry now is about most businesses who trade maybe 5 to 10% of their gross income. I think the only limit to that is that there aren't enough trade exchanges. So I'm hoping there will be more trade exchanges and more liquidity. I also see many more professional owners moving in. If you will, the plaid suit group is moving out, and younger professional owners are moving in. It just seems some of the old boys are leaving, and some of the newer guys are looking at this like it's more of a professional industry, more like the banking industry."

Steve White, Cascade Trade Association: " I think we should at least triple that number. I think we are going to start seeing our growth here anytime soon.

Scott Whitmer, The Exchange; IRTA: "We've seen this industry in the last 15 years grow each year, and I believe that will continue. I think it will continue at a faster percentage because of the communication tools available, with E-mail, with the Internet, potential common currency being developed."

15. BARTER IN THE YEAR 2020 **131**

By the year 2020 the retail barter industry will only be 60 years old. It's safe to say that the industry we see now will only be remotely related to the industry in 25 years. Once again, here's the thoughts of some industry professionals.

Duncan Banner, BXI: "I couldn't even imagine, but if the industry still exists, I would imagine that it would be melded into financial institutions as a financial instrument and have a very serious role, in the same way that countries do countertrade, it may be that large corporations now will countertrade, and even smaller businesses will countertrade and use it as a financial tool.

Mike Baer, ITEX: "We look for some real market penetration where barter is widely accepted with 40 to 50% of all small business owners participating. ITEX will be a major national and international currency."

Perry Constantinides, Barter Systems, Inc. Kensington, MD.: "I would guess 10% of all businesses will be in barter. And I think if that's the case, that we're all going to be extremely large."

Lois Dale, Barter Advantage Inc.: "I think it could go easily to 10% of all businesses."

Douglas Dagenais, Barter Corp.: "In 25 years, I think it will evolve much like the banking system. It will be a very normal practice. And I think it will also take on new international dimensions as the whole global market place evolves. So, whereas right now many companies are not attuned to the global marketplace, they will be in 25 years. Right now, there's very little interaction between barter companies in other countries outside the U.S., although they exist. In 25 years, I think that's going to be much, much stronger."

Keith Galuten, S.G.D. International Corp.: "It should definitely be at least 50% of the world economy. I mean, it's a huge percentage now. We have all these third-world nations that don't have any

currency, or any currency that has value. Because of that, they still
have resources, natural resources, that have value. Basically, currency only came about to represent your inventory."

Nelson Guyer, San Diego Barter: "I foresee about 80% of all small
and micro businesses being involved in barter. So that gives it a
pretty awesome growth potential."

Chris Haddawy, Barter Business Network: "I don't know if it'll
ever get to more than 15 to 20%. I think once too large a percentage of the business population is doing it, you lose the competitive
advantage. All of a sudden, it's just like cash, which people envi-
sion in barter as being a good thing. Well, I don't think it is a good
thing, because people have no reason to do it anymore. It being
different than cash and being an alternative payment method and
being something not everyone's doing is what gives a company its
competitive edge. If everyone's doing it, then the company has no
competitive advantage over the other businesses in the area."

Bill Jeffery, Barter Business Exchange: "Maybe 10%."

Tom McDowell, NATE: "I think we're going to see such a dramatic change in the monetary systems of the world that I don't know
what effect that's going to play on barter, when we go to electronic money as opposed to cash."

Timothy Ritchie, Merchant Trade Inc.: "Maybe as many as 25% of
the businesses will be using barter.

Mark Servatius, Allied Barter Corp.: "I'd like to see trade
exchanges on corners like banks."

Rachel Taylor, Barter Systems: "Well, 20% of all businesses—that's
pretty close to my projection."

Steve White, Cascade Trade: "In 25 years, I'm going to really relate
it to how credit cards got established or ATM machines. Myself, I
still don't have an ATM card; it's still a monster to me in a way. I
think I'm somewhat typical but a little more paranoid than the
average guy. So in 25 years, I really believe 50% of the business
population will be somehow related. Well, I think costs are going
to have to come down. It's going to be free to get in, just like a credit card is now. You're not going to pay a 10% service fee; it's going
to be maybe 5%, something like that. It's going to wrap right down

to what a credit card processing is. And that's where the industry will have to start going. It's too damn expensive for people to pay $500 and then 10%. We're not making any money charging those fees, because we're still in the infancy of the market.

Scott Whitmer, The Exchange; IRTA: "I think it really depends on the financial world as to whether the banks and Wall Street, how interested they get and how soon they become involved in the barter industry. They're of course looking at us right now. If they get involved, it could explode in the near future. I don't think in 25 years from now we're going to see that explosion; I think we'll see that tremendous growth in the next five years. I think it could easily be 10%."

16. WHY JOIN NOW?

If barter is still very much in a development stage and has such a bright future, why should I join now? We compare that question to people ten years ago saying 'Why should I get a computer now when they get better every year?' Some of those people are still waiting for computers to get perfect—and of course they never will.

In the case of trading, those getting involved now will in almost every case see their business become more profitable because of their involvement. They will become better traders and learn who they want to deal with. They will establish ties within exchanges that will allow them to get many of the better items that come along. The bottom line is, we know of no good reasons to wait.

7

RESOURCES

"NATE and IRTA are both excellent organizations, and we have benefitted from both greatly. What we find at IRTA is we learn quite a bit, and we're able to meet and develop new business opportunities. Whereas NATE is a bit more practical. More emphasis is put on the basics of the business. IRTA has helped us grow and learn more about the media and corporate trading sign-ups."

Bob Bagga,
Barter Business Exchange
Toronto, Canada

IRTA & NATE ⒔
The Conscience Of The Industry

The barter industry is indeed fortunate to have two active trade associations. As noted earlier, the International Reciprocal Trade Association, IRTA, is the oldest, having been founded in 1979. The National Association of Trade Exchanges, NATE, was formed in 1984 by a splinter group of IRTA members. In general, NATE members tend to be independent, locally owned exchanges. IRTA, the larger of the two organizations, has two distinct parts: the regular IRTA members who are generally either ITEX or BXI franchises or locally owned exchanges; and corporate traders that belong to the Corporate Trade Council. Here are some members thoughts on the two organizations:

Lisa Peters, Trade Systems Interchange: "We are members of both NATE and IRTA. They're very different organizations. IRTA has the Corporate Trade Council, so at least a third of the effort, a third of the conferences at a convention, are geared to a corporate trade. And they have a different perspective on things than retail trade exchanges do. There are a number of members who are franchise operations, so their focus is a little bit different, their problems and concerns are slightly different than mine as an independent operator. About two-thirds of the membership at IRTA are people with whom I don't have as much in common as I do with other independents. But there are some really, really wonderful exchanges in IRTA and I always enjoy seeing them and I benefit greatly from the conventions.

"In NATE, our membership is primarily independent trade exchanges for the most part. We live and breathe the same game. We have similar problems, circumstances, we share freely with each other. None of us is going to pro-actively try to assimilate all the other trade exchanges. When I go to an IRTA convention, there is a franchise operation that is unabashedly promoting its takeover of the barter industry. While I am not intimidated by that, it is a distraction. For me, NATE is a less stressful organization in that regard.

Bob Meyers, *Barter News*: "The professionalism is growing. There's a cadre now of people, and you're able to come to these conventions and pick up enormous amounts of good solid information on how to go out and start an exchange or develop your exchange.

This wasn't available 15, 18 years ago."

Bob Bagga, Barter Business Exchange: "NATE and IRTA are both excellent organizations, and we have benefitted from both greatly. What we find at IRTA is we learn quite a bit, and we're able to meet and develop new business opportunities. Whereas NATE is a bit more practical. More emphasis is put on the basics of the business. IRTA has helped us grow and learn more about the media and corporate trading sign-ups."

Mike Baer, ITEX: "Each of these organizations have done our industry a great service with ethics committees and standards. IRTA, having a few more years under its belt has really gone the extra mile in terms of lobbying congress to make sure there's the correct type of oversights, registration, licensing, testing of people to get into the industry and setting up accounting procedures within the industry."

Bruce Kamm, ITEX: "We work with IRTA all the time. People call into IRTA to find out which barter company should I talk to, which is a good exchange. We get leads and referrals from them. There's a lot of interaction."

Lois Dale, Barter Advantage Inc.: "Being a member of the board of directors of both NATE and IRTA at different times—I was vice president at one point in IRTA—I just feel NATE is much more down to earth and a friendlier group."

Scott Whitmer, The Exchange; IRTA: "Paul [Suplizio-CEO, IRTA] is very successful in attracting the corporate trade companies to become involved. As a result, we're seeing more interaction between retail trade exchanges trading with some of the larger corporate trade exchanges for things like Howard Johnson scrip and national advertising and things that have been available at a retail level before. That's why the IRTA conventions have been so productive and so important in recent years—because of the amount of corporate trade companies and retailers becoming involved, like Woolworth."

Tom McDowell, NATE: "My biggest success story is really more a NATE story than a barter story. NATE has always been driven by the notion that if we share with each other, we all gain from it. A lot of us who started NATE were in IRTA. We developed from our very first meeting an attitude, policy, that if you're not here to share what you know, both your successes and your failures, this isn't the group to be in. We have competitors in the same city who will get up on the same panel and talk about their compensation plans, their marketing plans, their successes, their failures, what they do. They've reached the point where they're not afraid of the competition anymore. They realize it's better for the whole industry, for all of us to grow and become successful, than to try and keep it a secret. The other difference is NATE is really a haven for independent trade exchanges. We focus on the independents, we focus on their profitability. Our goal is to put on events and do things that help make our members more profitable and more successful."

DIRECTORIES 134

The directory of retail and corporate barter companies on the following pages is not a complete listing of barter companies in the U.S., but rather a sampling. Generally, the companies listed here have responded to our faxed questionnaireand provided their own information. More complete directories are published by *Barter News* and by *The Operator*.

While the publishers of this book have dealt with many of the exchanges listed in this directory, we have not dealt with them all. Therefore, we make no guarantees as to the business worthiness of these companies.

ADVERTISING 135

Following the directory is a section featuring advertising of barter organizations from across the United Sates and Canada. This section is an excellent source of professionals in the barter industry who can assist you in your barter needs. We appreciate your patronage of their businesses.

United States Retail Barter Organizations

(This is not a complete listing, but rather a sampling)

ALABAMA

The Trade Exchange Council

107 Comer Circle
Daphne AL
36546-7640 USA
Contact: John Riva
Phone: 334-621-6842
Fax: 334-621-6842
E Mail:
Organ.: **IRTA**
Members: Founded:

ARKANSAS

Bartercard, Inc

822 Cumberland #1
Little Rock AR
72202 USA
Contact: Kenn Flemmons
Phone: 501-376-2278
Fax: 501-376-1906
E Mail:
Organ.: **NATE**
Members: Founded: **1981**

ARIZONA

Barter Group

8700 E. Vaia De Ventura #205
Scottsdale AZ
85258 USA
Contact: Shari Baker
Phone: 602-443-0322
Fax: 602-483-7241
E Mail:
Organ.: **NATE**
Members: Founded:

BXI Phoenix

6560 N. Scottsdale Road, Suite
Scottsdale AZ
85203 USA
Contact: Lee & Terry Brandfass
Phone: 602-951-2929
Fax: 602-951-6949
E Mail:
Organ.: **NATE**
Members: Founded:

CALIFORNIA

America's Barter Network

1946 Mentone Blvd.
Mentone CA
92359 USA
Contact: Robert Bechtold
Phone: 909-794-8114
Fax: 909-389-1288
E Mail:
Organ.: **IRTA**
Members: **387**   Founded: **1993**

American Commerce Exchange

10556 Riverside Dr.
Toluca Lake CA
91602 USA
Contact: Mark Tracy
Phone: 818-769-2223
Fax: 818-769-6664
E Mail:
Organ.: **NATE**
Members: **500**   Founded: **1982**

American Trade Association

Box 150285
San Rafael CA
94915 USA
Contact: David Wallach
Phone: 415-883-3242
Fax: 415-883-2657
E Mail:
Organ.: **IRTA NATE**
Members: Founded:

Barter Connection

1414 Soquel Ave., #102
Santa Cruz CA
95062 USA
Contact: Susan Williams
Phone: 408 -469-9001
Fax: 408-469-9008
E Mail:
Organ.: **IRTA NATE**
Members: **550**   Founded: **1986**

Barter Exchange

1600 N. Arrowhead Av., Ste. 1
San Bernardino CA
92005 USA
Contact: Tony de la Torre
Phone: 909-881-6131
Fax: 909-881-6133
E Mail:
Organ.:
Members: **150**   Founded: **1985**

Bay Area & Hawaii Barter Exchange

582 Folsom St.
San Francisco CA
94105 USA
Contact: Steve Goldbloom
Phone: 415-777-0123
Fax: 415-777-1012
E Mail:
Organ.: **IRTA NATE**
Members: **850**   Founded: **1984**

Business Exchange International, Inc - BXI

333 N. Glen Oaks Blvd
Burbank CA
91502 USA
Contact: Stephen Friedland
Phone: 818-563-4966
Fax: 818-563-4965
E Mail:
Organ.: **NATE**
Members: **25,000**   Founded: **1960**

BXI Central Northern California

3388 Brittan Ave., Ste. 9
San Carlos CA
94070 USA
Contact: P. Ronald Keister
  Phone: 415-761-9300
    Fax: 916-802-9473
  E Mail:
  Organ.: **IRTA**
Members: Founded:

BXI Inland Valley

1173 North Dixie Drive, Suite
San Dimas CA
91773 USA
Contact: Peter Brooks
  Phone: 909-592-7727
    Fax: 909-599-1802
  E Mail:
  Organ.:
Members: **650**   Founded: **1990**

BXI No. Calif. Member Services

2355 Oakland Rd.
San Jose CA
95131-1415 USA
Contact: Rick Owens
  Phone: 408-474-0400
    Fax: 408-474-0414
  E Mail:
  Organ.: **IRTA**
Members: Founded:

BXI of Orange County

18377 Beach Blvd., #217
Huntington Beach CA
92648 USA
Contact: Ilan Ben- Yosef
  Phone: 714-847-5477
    Fax: 714-847-4276
  E Mail:
  Organ.: **NATE**
Members: Founded: **1962**

BXI of Santa Barbara and Ventura

2437 Grand Avenue, Suite 279
Ventura CA
93003 USA
Contact: Ryan Van Trees
  Phone: 805-659-6880
    Fax: 805-659-0743
  E Mail: ven bxi@fishnet.com
  Organ.: **IRTA**
Members: **600**   Founded: **1987**

BXI San Diego

4045 Bonita Rd., Ste. 201
Bonita CA
91902 USA
Contact: Duncan Banner
  Phone: 619-472-2929
    Fax: 619-280-1595
  E Mail:
  Organ.: **IRTA NATE**
Members: **650**   Founded: **1960**

BXI San Francisco
2800/370 Hilltop Mall Road
Richmond CA
94806 USA
Contact: Bob Dorenstreich
  Phone: 510-758-0181
    Fax: 510-758-0182
E Mail:
Organ.: **IRTA NATE**
Members: Founded:

Global Exchange Network, Inc.
1920 Main Street, Suite 200
Irvine CA
92714 USA
Contact: Sondra Ames
  Phone: 714-756-5665
    Fax: 714-756-5670
E Mail:
Organ.: **IRTA**
Members: Founded: **1974**

BXI South Riverside Co.
28362 Vicent Moraga Dr. #A-1
Temecula CA
92590 USA
Contact: Paul Orozco
  Phone: 909-695-4774
    Fax: 619-698-7850
E Mail:
Organ.:
Members: **400**   Founded: **1993**

ITEX San Diego
827 West Washington, Ste. 240
San Diego CA
92103 USA
Contact: Don Schmidt
  Phone: 619-757-9327
    Fax: 619-757-1767
E Mail:
Organ.: **IRTA**
Members: **200**   Founded: **1989**

BXI West Los Angeles
600 South Carson Avenue, #312
Los Angeles CA
90036 USA
Contact: Alan Zimmelman
  Phone: 213-935-2929
    Fax: 213-935-2934
E Mail:
Organ.: **NATE**
Members: **600**   Founded: **1987**

ITEX Sunrise
3535 Riviera Dr.
San Diego CA
92019 USA
Contact: Helene Erenson
  Phone: 619-581-2807
    Fax: 619-270-0757
E Mail:
Organ.:
Members: **100**   Founded: **1996**

Itrade Inc.
112 Shipley
San Francisco CA
94107 USA
Contact: Caleb Chaundy
Phone: 415-541-9400
Fax: 415-979-0901
E Mail: caleb@itrade.com
Organ.:
Members: Founded:

M.E. Nelson Company, Inc.
8512 Templeman Rd.
Forestville CA
95436 USA
Contact: Ron Friedwald
Phone: 707-887-9288
Fax: 707-887-9582
E Mail:
Organ.: NATE
Members: Founded:

Master Trade Barter Systems
15814 Winchester Blvd., Ste. 103
Los Gatos CA
95030 USA
Contact: Francy Nadezad
Phone: 408-354-8173
Fax: 408-354-4493
E Mail:
Organ.: IRTA
Members: Founded: 1992

San Diego Barter

San Diego CA
USA
Contact: Nelson Guyer
Phone: 619-587-3938
Fax: 619-587-3918
E Mail:
Organ.: NATE
Members: 150   Founded: 1995

Trade American Card
777 South Main, Suite 77
Orange CA
92668 USA
Contact: Michael Ames
Phone: 714-543-8283
Fax: 714-541-3290
E Mail: tacbarter
Organ.: NATE
Members: 2,500   Founded: 1970

Trade Club Exchange
7717 Garden Grove Blvd.
Garden Grove CA
92641 USA
Contact: Joe Hill
Phone: 714-891-8497
Fax: 714-895-2895
E Mail: www.bartertce.com
Organ.:
Members: 1,750   Founded: 1993

Trade Systems Interchange

5350 Commerce Blvd., Suite C,
Rohnert Park CA
94928-1652 USA
Contact: Lisa Peters
  Phone: 707-585-7722
  Fax: 707-585-6231
E Mail:
Organ.: **IRTA NATE**
Members: **500**   Founded: **1981**

Answertech

1703 E. 18th St., Bldg. 3
Loveland CO
80538 USA
Contact: Scott D. Meyers
  Phone: 970-679-8787
  Fax: 970-667-0666
E Mail:
Organ.: **IRTA**
Members: Founded:

Tradeworld

851 E. Hamilton Ave. Ste. 110
Campbell CA
95008 USA
Contact: Roger Pitkin
  Phone: 408-371-8101
  Fax: 408-371-4703
E Mail:
Organ.:
Members: **2,000**   Founded: **1986**

ITEX Denver

13741 E. Rice Place, #106
Aurora CO
80015 USA
Contact: Kay Thompson
  Phone: 303-561-0836
  Fax: 303-561-1404
E Mail:
Organ.: **IRTA**
Members: Founded: **1984**

COLORADO

ABC of the Rocky Mountains Inc.

2591 Airport Rd.
Colorado Springs CO
80910 USA
Contact: Joe White
  Phone: 800-498-7243
  Fax: 719-578-9994
E Mail:
Organ.: **NATE**
Members: Founded: **1996**

Rocky Mountain Tradecard

2450 Central Avenue, Ste. P-5
Boulder CO
80301 USA
Contact: Debbie Schramm
  Phone: 303-443-2106
  Fax: 303-440-8881
E Mail:
Organ.: **IRTA**
Members: Founded: **1992**

Tele Trade Int'l.
17009 CarrAve–Lower Level
Parker CO
80134 USA
Contact: Gary Lasater
Phone: 303-840-7172
Fax: 303-840-7173
E Mail:
Organ.: **IRTA**
Members: Founded:

CONNECTICUT

Barter Business Unlimited Inc,
Box 2912
Bristol CT
06011-2912 USA
Contact: Deborah A. Lombardi
Phone: 203-676-1986
Fax: 203-676-2730
E Mail:
Organ.: **IRTA NATE**
Members: Founded:

Barter Network, Inc.
53 River St.
Milford CT
06460
Contact: Ray Bastarache
Phone: 203-874-8962
Fax: 203-874-3674
E Mail:
Organ.: **IRTA**
Members: **4,600**   Founded: **1985**

Exchange Enterprises
50 Washington St.
Norwalk CT
06854 USA
Contact: Mike Hurworth
Phone: 203-866-8848
Fax: 203-852-1079
E Mail:
Organ.: **IRTA NATE**
Members: **450**   Founded: **1984**

Genesis International Ltd.
75 Holly Hill Lane
Greenwich CT
06830 USA
Contact: Edward Eglowsky
Phone: 203-629-3355
Fax: 203-629-3598
E Mail:
Organ.: **IRTA**
Members: Founded:

DISTRICT OF COLUMBIA

Allied Barter Corporation
4830 43rd St. NW
Washington DC
20016-4019 USA
Contact: Mark Servatius
Phone: 202-364-4222
Fax: 202-364-0221
E Mail:
Organ.: **IRTA**
Members: **131**   Founded: **1995**

DELAWARE

Delaware Barter Corporation

2500 West 4th St., Suite 2
Wilmington DE
19805 USA
Contact: Michael Skibicki
  Phone: 302-652-8937
    Fax: 302-652-8643
E Mail:
Organ.: **IRTA NATE**
Members: **1,000**   Founded: **1993**

FLORIDA

Alternative Capital Resources

2637 syndelle St.
Sarasota FL
34237 USA
Contact: Arthur R. Seaborne
  Phone: 800-954-8122
    Fax: 813-954-5854
E Mail:
Organ.: **IRTA**
Members: Founded:

American Barter Company

1900 S. Harbor City Blvd, #221
Melbourne FL
32901 USA
Contact: Alan Dodson
  Phone: 407-728-7287
    Fax: 407-951-9666
E Mail:
Organ.: **NATE**
Members: Founded: **1991**

Barter Center of South Florida

4801 So. University Dr.
Davie FL
33328 USA
Contact: Mike Sazzolare
  Phone: 305-927-7447
    Fax:
E Mail:
Organ.:
Members: **2,100**   Founded:

Barter Worldwide USA

16116 Northglenn Dr.
Tampa FL
33618 USA
Contact: Jeff F. Horner
  Phone: 813-963-1159
    Fax: 813 -963-5383
E Mail:
Organ.: **IRTA**
Members: **3,500**   Founded: **1989**

BXI of Central Florida, Inc.

722 Commerce Circle
Longwood FL
32750 USA
Contact: Josh Ducios
  Phone: 407-834-1938
    Fax: 407-834-6549
E Mail:
Organ.:
Members: **200**   Founded:

Coastal Trade Exchange
1401 20th St.
Vero Beach FL
32960 USA
Contact: Charles Hearnshaw
  Phone: 407-778-0833
  Fax: 407-778-1033
E Mail:
Organ.: **IRTA NATE**
Members: **500**   Founded: **1993**

Florida Business & Trade Exchange
8442 S. Federal Highway
Port St. Lucie FL
34952 USA
Contact: Maurice Warren
  Phone: 407-340-1777
  Fax: 407-878-3164
E Mail:
Organ.: **NATE**
Members: Founded: **1991**

Florida Trade Association, Inc
2660 N.E. First St.
Pompano Beach FL
33062 USA
Contact: Michael J. Yolich
  Phone: 407-941-0414
  Fax: 305-941-4173
E Mail:
Organ.: **IRTA**
Members: Founded: **1982**

Gulf Coast Trade Exchange, Inc.
Box 8125
Pensacola FL
32505 USA
Contact: Bob Crumpton
  Phone: 904-434-5278
  Fax: 904-433-0832
E Mail:
Organ.: **NATE**
Members: Founded: **1977**

International Bankers and Exchangers
3111-21 Mahan Dr., #118
Tallahassee FL
32308 USA
Contact: J. Sid Raehm
  Phone: 904-656-3404
  Fax: 904-942-1496
E Mail:
Organ.: **IRTA NATE**
Members: Founded:

International Barter Exchange IBE
4000 S. Tamiami Trail, #408
Sarasota FL
34276-3188 USA
Contact: Ron & Mary Unger
  Phone: 941-925-7776
  Fax: 941-925-8150
E Mail:
Organ.: **NATE**
Members: Founded:

ITEX West Palm Beach
927 Turner Quay
Jupiter FL
33458 USA
Contact: Hal J. Henry
Phone: 407-747-6999
Fax: 407-746-2317
E Mail:
Organ.: **IRTA**
Members: **180**   Founded: **1983**

Nat'l. Commerce Exchange of Tampa Bay
14011–66th St. North
Largo FL
34641 USA
Contact: Tom Archibald
Phone: 813-539-8719
Fax: 813-531-4678
E Mail:
Organ.: **IRTA**
Members: **800**   Founded: **1982**

POA Trade Exchange
5333 Old Winter Garden Rd.
Orlando FL
32811 USA
Contact: Jim Matalone
Phone: 407-298-6410
Fax: 407-297-8176
E Mail:
Organ.: **IRTA**
Members: Founded:

The Exchange
5072 Edgewater Drive
Orlando FL
32810 USA
Contact: Scott Whitmer
Phone: 407-291-2952
Fax: 407-293-5472
E Mail:
Organ.: **IRTA**
Members: **1,350**   Founded: **1982**

The Trade Exchange
2920 Kensington St.
Stuart FL
34997 USA
Contact: Wayne Stemmer
Phone: 407-288-6263
Fax: 407-288-6446
E Mail:
Organ.: **IRTA**
Members: Founded:

The Trade Exchange
14925 US Hwy 19
Hudson FL
34667 USA
Contact: Chad Reid
Phone: 813-868-7151
Fax: 813-868-6824
E Mail:
Organ.: **IRTA**
Members: Founded:

Trade Exchange of America–Florida

1408 S.W. 3rd St., Ste. 7
Pompano Beach FL
33069-4709 USA
Contact:
Phone: 305-781-5000
Fax: 305-943-7279
E Mail:
Organ.: **IRTA**
Members: Founded:

Trade Express

304 Wymore Rd., Apt 101
Altamonte Springs FL
32714 USA
Contact: Ruthanne Milam
Phone: 407-786-0954
Fax: 407-786-0954
E Mail:
Organ.: **IRTA**
Members: Founded:

Trade Source

80 SW 8th St–20th Floor
Miami FL
33130 USA
Contact: Alan Wolfson
Phone: 305-374-4666
Fax: 305-373-8744
E Mail:
Organ.: **NATE**
Members: Founded:

Travel Recovery Systems

25 S. E. 2nd Ave. Ste 1131
Miami FL
33131 USA
Contact: Herb Lowenthal
Phone: 305-358-0665
Fax: 305-358-2242
E Mail:
Organ.: **IRTA**
Members: Founded: **1966**

GEORGIA

BXI of Georgia Inc.

1105 West Ave., Suite A
Conyers GA
30207 USA
Contact: Frank Scott
Phone: 404-929-8500
Fax: 404-760-0800
E Mail:
Organ.: **NATE**
Members: Founded:

ITEX Atlanta

2080 Peachtree Industrial Ct.
Atlanta GA
30341 USA
Contact: Jule Gulley
Phone: 770- 458-6135
Fax: 770 458-6418
E Mail:
Organ.: **IRTA**
Members: Founded: **1987**

The Savannah Trade Exchange

7505 Waters Ave.
Savannah GA
31328 USA
Contact: Joe Moran
  Phone: 912-355-2555
    Fax: 912-355-3435
E Mail:
Organ.: **NATE**
Members: **500**   Founded:

Trade Partners International, Inc.

7992 Rockbridge Rd.
Lithonia GA
30058 USA
Contact: Cyndee Parker
  Phone: 404-484-7002
    Fax: 404-484-7006
E Mail:
Organ.: **NATE**
Members: Founded:

Tradebank International, Inc.

4220 Pleasantdale Rd.
Atlanta GA
30340 USA
Contact: John Davis
  Phone: 770-446-7600
    Fax: 770-446-9595
E Mail: bank@tradebank-intl.co
Organ.: **NATE**
Members: **2,500**   Founded: **1987**

IOWA

Heartland Barter Exchange

Box 936
Cedar Falls IA
50613 USA
Contact: Roy Tucker
  Phone: 319-266-7900
    Fax: 319-266-6503
E Mail:
Organ.: **NATE**
Members: Founded:

ILLINOIS

Advantage Barter Corp.

Box 203
Palos Heights IL
60463 USA
Contact: Len Cooper
  Phone: 708-873-0435
    Fax:
E Mail:
Organ.: **IRTA**
Members: Founded:

Art of Barter Inc.

303 E Wacker Dr. #830
Chicago IL
60601 USA
Contact: Ron Szekeres
  Phone: 312-616-1660
    Fax: 312-920-0200
E Mail:
Organ.: **NATE**
Members: **3,000**   Founded: **1991**

Barter Corp.
18 W 100 22nd St.
Oakbrook Terrace IL
60181 USA
Contact: Susan Groenwald x104
Phone: 800-589-2278
Fax: 708-953-8101
E Mail:
Organ.: **IRTA NATE**
Members: **3,000**   Founded: **1980**

Commercial Barter of Illinois
Box 345
Plainfield IL
60544 USA
Contact: Sid Freedman
Phone: 815-439-0070
Fax: 815-436-8992
E Mail:
Organ.: **NATE**
Members: Founded:

Fun Guides
175 Olde Half Day Rd.
Lincolnshire IL
60069 USA
Contact: Rich Rosenbaum
Phone: 708-883-9944
Fax: 708-883-9949
E Mail:
Organ.: **NATE**
Members: Founded:

Illinois Trade Association
4208 Commercial Way
Glenview IL
60025 USA
Contact: Jack Schacht
Phone: 847-390-6000
Fax: 847-390-6226
E Mail:
Organ.: **IRTA NATE**
Members: **4,200**   Founded: **1983**

Midwest Trade Exchange
2300 Green Bay Rd.
North Chicago IL
60064 USA
Contact: Sue Monkman
Phone: 708-689-2300
Fax: 708-689-2309
E Mail:
Organ.: **NATE**
Members: Founded:

INDIANA

Touch Talk
1800 N. Meridian, Ste. 401
Indianapolis IN
46202 USA
Contact: Bob Day
Phone: 317-921-0247
Fax: 317-921-0249
E Mail:
Organ.: **IRTA**
Members: Founded: **1989**

Trade Secrets Exchange

2016 Vance Ave.
Ft. Wayne IN
46805 USA
Contact: Larraine Olsen Conrad
Phone: 219-483-0653
Fax:
E Mail:
Organ.: **IRTA**
Members: Founded:

New Orleans Trade Exchange

Box 19181
New Orleans LA
70179 USA
Contact: Harry Perret
Phone: 504-486-9500
Fax: 504-486-9528
E Mail:
Organ.: **NATE**
Members: Founded: **1977**

KANSAS

Kansas Trade Exchange

438 South Greenwood
Wichita KS
67211 USA
Contact: Hayes G. Crenshaw
Phone: 316-264-7497
Fax: 316-264-7437
E Mail:
Organ.: **NATE**
Members: Founded:

MASS.

Barter Connections, Inc

822 Boylston St.
Chestnut Hill MA
02167 USA
Contact: Kenneth C. Barron
Phone: 617-738-8800
Fax: 617-738-9655
E Mail:
Organ.: **IRTA**
Members: **2,000**   Founded: **1979**

LOUISIANA

Crescent City Trade Exchange

5500 Prytania--Box 211
New Orleans LA
70130 USA
Contact: Tanya Galdamez
Phone: 504-529-4646
Fax: 504-522-1719
E Mail:
Organ.: **NATE**
Members: **500**   Founded: **1994**

BarterMax, Inc

1600 Executive Center-2nd Fl.,
Sharon MA
02116 USA
Contact: Al Kafka
Phone: 617-769-3400
Fax: 508-660-3070
E Mail:
Organ.: **IRTA NATE**
Members: **1,400**   Founded: **1982**

Boston Business Exchange, Inc. (BBX)

196 Boston Ave., Ste. 3400
Medford MA
02155 USA
Contact: Gary Oshmy
Phone: 617 395-9100
Fax: 617 395-5949
E Mail: bbxgary@aol.com
Organ.: **IRTA**
Members: **800**   Founded: **1984**

Business & Professional Trade Exchange, Inc

P. O. Box 168
E. Longmeadow MA
01028 USA
Contact: Lawrence Solomon
Phone: 413-525-3346
Fax: 413-525 -2071
E Mail:
Organ.:
Members: **800**   Founded: **1980**

BXI Boston

4 Albion Place
Boston MA
02129 USA
Contact: John Falletti
Phone: 617-242-8909
Fax: 617-242-3254
E Mail:
Organ.: **NATE**
Members: Founded:

The Barter Club

34 Main Street Extension
Plymouth MA
02360 USA
Contact: Rich Tribuna
Phone: 508-747-5255
Fax: 508-746-4415
E Mail:
Organ.: **NATE**
Members: Founded:

Unlimited Business Exchange (UBE)

926 Eastern Av.
Malden MA
02148 USA
Contact: Kenneth Meharg
Phone: 617-322-9009
Fax: 617-321-4443
E Mail:
Organ.: **NATE**
Members: **950**   Founded: **1980**

MARYLAND

Baltimore Trade Exchange

Box 3567
Baltimore MD
21214 USA
Contact: Mary Anne Rishebarger
Phone: 410-254-4018
Fax: 410-426-4501
E Mail:
Organ.: **IRTA**
Members: .   Founded:

Barter Systems, Inc. BSI
3717 Decatur Avenue, 2nd Level
Kensington MD
20895 USA
Contact: Perry Constantinides
Phone: 301-949-4900
Fax: 301-949-0142
E Mail: info@bartersys.com
Organ.: **NATE**
Members: **1,500**   Founded: **1976**

Creative Barter Network
Box 338
Arnold MD
21012 USA
Contact: Gail Yates
Phone: 410-974-4904
Fax: 410-974-4431
E Mail:
Organ.: **NATE**
Members: **300**   Founded: **1992**

MAINE

The Trade Exchange, Inc.
27 Gorham Rd. Ste L
Scarbough ME
04074-8381 USA
Contact: L. Bill Austin
Phone: 207-883-5577
Fax: 207-883-1070
E Mail: barter@maine.com
Organ.: **IRTA**
Members: **500**   Founded: **1977**

MICHIGAN

Metro Trading Association
555 Oliver St.
Troy MI
48084 USA
Contact: Michael Mercier
Phone: 810-244-0000
Fax: 810-244-0012
E Mail:
Organ.: **NATE**
Members: Founded: **1978**

Midwest Business Exchange, ltd
5111 Miller Rd., #11B
Kalamazoo MI
49001 USA
Contact: Jerry Howell
Phone: 616-344-8800
Fax: 616-344-8522
E Mail:
Organ.: **NATE**
Members: Founded: **1980**

Trade Exchange of America
23200 Coolidge Hwy.
Oak Park MI
48237 USA
Contact: Fred Detwiler
Phone: 810-544-1350
Fax: 810-544-1546
E Mail: jpltrader@ring.com
Organ.:
Members: **5,000**   Founded: **1978**

Trade Network Inc

Box 700
Haslett MI
48840-0700 USA
Contact: Gary Kay
  Phone: 517-886-8900
    Fax: 517-886-8915
E Mail:
Organ.: **NATE**
Members: Founded: **1991**

MINNESOTA

Summit Trade Exchange

216 W. Superior St. Skywalk
Duluth MN
55802 USA
Contact: Bob Boone
  Phone: 218-722-0258
    Fax: 218-722-8747
E Mail:
Organ.: **NATE**
Members: Founded:

MISSOURI

American Exchange Network

105 East Gregory Blvd.
Kansas City MO
64114 USA
Contact: Harold Rice
  Phone: 816-444-7927
    Fax: 816-523-5444
E Mail:
Organ.: **IRTA NATE**
Members: **1,800**   Founded:

ITEX St. Louis

11710 Administration Dr. #26
St. Louis MO
63146 USA
Contact: Karen S. Hoffman
  Phone: 314-432-8989
    Fax: 314-432-5620
E Mail:
Organ.: **IRTA**
Members: **380**   Founded: **1987**

Maxcard Inc.

1730 East Republic Dr., #A207
Springfield MO
65804 USA
Contact: Rich Johnson
  Phone: 417-889-2273
    Fax: 417-882-5860
E Mail:
Organ.: **NATE**
Members: Founded:

National Commercial Exchange

106 Four Season Center, #107B
Chesterfield MO
63017 USA
Contact: Richard Harris
  Phone: 314-469-1919
    Fax: 314-469-2876
E Mail:
Organ.: **NATE**
Members: **700**   Founded: **1980**

Premier Radio Network
One Cityplace Dr., #530
St. Louis MO
63141 USA
Contact: Steve Lehman
  Phone: 314-377-5300
    Fax: 314-377-5320
  E Mail:
  Organ.: **NATE**
Members: Founded:

Barter Business Exchange
Box 10528
Raleigh NC
27605-0528 USA
Contact: Maurya Purcell
  Phone: 919-772-2202
    Fax: 919-772-2629
  E Mail:
  Organ.: **IRTA**
Members: Founded:

ITEX New Hampshire
1817 Woodbury Av.
Portsmouth NH
03801 USA
Contact: Richard E. Crabtree
  Phone: 603-436-4603
    Fax: 603-436-2992
  E Mail:
  Organ.: **IRTA**
Members: Founded:

American Barter Company Inc.
467 Green Tree Rd.
Sewell NJ
08080 USA
Contact: Thomas Shipman
  Phone: 609-589-6731
    Fax: 609-589-2833
  E Mail:
  Organ.: **IRTA**
Members: Founded: **1990**

Barter Pays! Inc.
522 Rt. 9 North, #175
Manalapan NJ
07726 USA
Contact: Faye Vitale
Phone: 908-364-4614
Fax: 908-901-9273
E Mail:
Organ.: **NATE**
Members: **400**   Founded: **1993**

Trade Works Inc
158 W. Clinton St.
Dover NJ
07801 USA
Contact: Richard Hurley
Phone: 201-366-6100
Fax: 201-366-6712
E Mail:
Organ.: **IRTA NATE**
Members: Founded:

NEVADA

Barter Business Network
5890 S. Virginia St.
Reno NV
89502 USA
Contact: Chris Haddawy
Phone: 702-826-1100
Fax: 702-826-8919
E Mail:
Organ.: **NATE**
Members: **350**   Founded: **1995**

BXI Reno/Tahoe
20 Hillcrest Drive, Suite C
Reno NV
89509 USA
Contact: Linda Rubendall
Phone: 702-829-2990
Fax: 702-829-2991
E Mail:
Organ.:
Members: **225**   Founded: **1986**

The Lodging Group
3395 S. Jones Blvd., Ste. 153
Las Vegas NV
89102 USA
Contact: D. Alan Clark
Phone: 702-737-0453
Fax: 702-737-1286
E Mail:
Organ.: **IRTA**
Members: Founded:

Western Barter ITEX
2001 Paridise
Las Vegas NV
89104 USA
Contact: David Heller
Phone: 702-796-5777
Fax: 702-796-0754
E Mail: itex@wizard.com
Organ.: **IRTA**
Members: **250**   Founded: **1991**

NEW YORK

American Barter Exchange

64 Division Av.
Levittown NY
11756 USA
Contact: Cheryl Mera
Phone: 516-520-0800
Fax: 516-520-0813
E Mail:
Organ.: **NATE**
Members: **750**   Founded: **1983**

Atwood Richards

99 Park Ave. 15th Fl.
New York NY
10016 USA
Contact: Moreton Binn
Phone: 212-490-1414
Fax: 212-661-8343
E Mail:
Organ.:
Members: Founded:

Barter Advantage, Inc

1751 Second Av.
New York NY
10028 USA
Contact: Lois Dale
Phone: 212-534-7500
Fax: 212-534-8145
E Mail:
Organ.: **NATE**
Members: **2,200**   Founded:

Barter Group Inc.

26 Garrigan Av.
Pleasantville NY
10570 USA
Contact: Steven J Nunes
Phone: 914-747-8527
Fax: 914-747-1428
E Mail:
Organ.: **NATE**
Members: Founded:

Barter Network Inc.

78 Main St.
Kings Park NY
11754 USA
Contact: Domenic Casillo
Phone: 516-269-0700
Fax: 516-269-9318
E Mail:
Organ.: **IRTA**
Members: **4,600**   Founded: **1985**

ITEX Metro

115 W. Jericho Turnpike
Huntington Station NY
11746 USA
Contact: Don Trooien
Phone: 516-351-4839
Fax: 516-351-4862
E Mail:
Organ.: **IRTA**
Members: **300**   Founded: **1989**

ITEX New York

126 East 37th St.
New York NY
10016 USA
Contact: Bruce Kamm
   Phone: 212-251-0300
   Fax: 212-251-0375
   E Mail: itex@ix.netcom.com
   Organ.: **IRTA**
Members: **550**   Founded: **1992**

Ithaca Hours

Box 6578
Ithaca NY
14851 USA
Contact: Paul Glover
   Phone: 607-272-4330
   Fax: 607-277-0801
   E Mail: ithacahour@aol.com
   Organ.:
Members: **1,500**   Founded: **1991**

Manhattan Barter Ltd.

17 Little West 12th St.
New York NY
10014 USA
Contact: Santiago Negroni
   Phone: 212-229-1600
   Fax: 212-727-9598
   E Mail:
   Organ.: **NATE**
Members: Founded:

National Commerce Exchange

400 Jericho Turnpike
Jericho NY
11753 USA
Contact: Dick Paer
   Phone: 516-935-2280
   Fax: 516-935-2316
   E Mail:
   Organ.: **NATE**
Members: Founded:

United States Barter Group

863 W. Hericho Trpk.
Smithtown NY
11787 USA
Contact: Ron Cusano Sr.
   Phone: 516-269-0700
   Fax: 516-269-9318
   E Mail:
   Organ.: **NATE**
Members: Founded:

Vista Media Inc.

64 Division Ave., Ste. 101
Levittown NY
11756-2995 USA
Contact: Mitchell Schultz
   Phone: 516-921-1148
   Fax: 516-921-1136
   E Mail:
   Organ.: **IRTA**
Members: Founded:

OHIO

American Trade Exchange Inc.

27801 Euclid Ave., #610
Cleveland OH
44132 USA
Contact: Tom McDowell
  Phone: 216-731-8030
    Fax: 216-731-7724
  E Mail:
  Organ.: **NATE**
Members: **475**   Founded: **1982**

BarterBoard

Box 293039
Kettering OH
45429 USA
Contact: Roger & Beverly Long
  Phone: 513-526-9757
    Fax: 513-435-5024
  E Mail:
  Organ.: **NATE**
Members: Founded:

National Association of Trade Exchanges NATE

27801 Euclid Ave., Ste 610
Cleveland OH
44132 USA
Contact: Tom McDowell
  Phone: 216-732-7171
    Fax: 216-732-7172
  E Mail:
  Organ.: **NATE**
Members: **109**   Founded: **1984**

Trade Exchange of America–Toledo

7858 W. Central
Toledo OH
43517-1530 USA
Contact:
  Phone: 419-843-2555
    Fax: 419-843-2073
  E Mail:
  Organ.: **IRTA**
Members: Founded:

OKLAHOMA

BXI Tulsa

4815 South Harvard, Suite 510
Tulsa OK
74135 USA
Contact: Alan, Trish Elias
  Phone: 918-749-2266
    Fax: 918-747-6768
  E Mail:
  Organ.: **NATE**
Members: Founded: **1980**

OREGON

ITEX Corporation

Box 2309
Portland OR
97208 USA
Contact: Michael T. Baer
  Phone: 800-225-4839
    Fax: 503-245-0748
  E Mail:
  Organ.: **IRTA**
Members: **30,000**   Founded: **1982**

Multimedia Access Company

822 NW Murray Blvd., Ste. 303
Portland OR
97299 USA
Contact: Terry L. Neal
  Phone: 503-245-6063
    Fax: 503-245-5868
  E Mail: gerald.pitts@itex.com
  Organ.: **IRTA**
Members: Founded:

Society of Trading Associates

261 E. Barnett
Medford OR
97501 USA
Contact: Donald E. McCoy III
  Phone: 503-776-0407
    Fax: 503-776-9804
  E Mail:
  Organ.: **IRTA**
Members: Founded:

PENNSYLVANIA

American Trade Services

42 W. Lancaster Av.
Ardmore PA
19003 USA
Contact: Howard Taylor
  Phone: 610-642-7000
    Fax: 610-642-7378
  E Mail:
  Organ.: **IRTA**
Members: Founded:

BXI Eastern Pennsylvania

Box 125
Wernersville PA
19565 USA
Contact: Jeff Burkhardt
  Phone: 610-678-2100
    Fax: 610-670-1160
  E Mail:
  Organ.: **IRTA**
Members: Founded: **1991**

Greenapple Barter Services

Box 101131
Pittsburgh PA
15237 USA
Contact: Michael Crane
  Phone: 412-369-7000
    Fax: 412-369-4801
  E Mail:
  Organ.: **NATE**
Members: Founded:

ITS Corp.

219 Sugartown Rd., Ste. P103
Wayne PA
19087 USA
Contact: Jess Kaufman
  Phone: 610-687-2929
    Fax: 610-687-6442
  E Mail:
  Organ.: **IRTA**
Members: Founded:

SOUTH CAROLINA

GSX Enterprises
210 East Hwy 90, Ste. 3
Little River SC
29566 USA
Contact: George Edwards
Phone: 803-249-0919
Fax: 803-280-0832
E Mail: gsxtrader@aol.com
Organ.: **IRTA**
Members: Founded:

IBG Grand Strand
201-E 1500 Hiway 17 North
Surfside Beach SC
29575 USA
Contact: Donna Johnson
Phone: 803-477-1501
Fax: 803-477-1800
E Mail:
Organ.: **IRTA**
Members: Founded:

International Barter Group
1766 Meeting St.
Charleston SC
29403 USA
Contact: George Fisette
Phone: 803-824-1435
Fax: 803-824-1438
E Mail: Gfisette@www.ibg-trad
Organ.: **IRTA**
Members: **1,000**   Founded: **1981**

TENNESSEE

A.S.K. Incorporated
5810 Ferguson Rd.
Memphis TN
38134 USA
Contact: David & Susan Cooper
Phone: 901-386-3269
Fax: 901-386-0170
E Mail:
Organ.: **NATE**
Members: Founded:

BXI Eastern Tennessee
7632 Clinton Highway
Powell TN
37849 USA
Contact: Ray Lipps
Phone: 615-947-9396
Fax: 615-947-6269
E Mail:
Organ.: **NATE**
Members: Founded:

Eagle Barter Exchange
6960 Lee Highway #105
Chattanooga TN
37421 USA
Contact: Johnny Eagle
Phone: 615-899-1001
Fax: 615-899-4940
E Mail:
Organ.: **NATE**
Members: Founded: **1993**

TEXAS

Amarillo Trade Exchange

2505 Lakeview #203
Amarillo TX
79109 USA
Contact: Wes Reitz
  Phone: 806-352-9665
    Fax: 806-352-4489
  E Mail: atx@amaonline.com
  Organ.: **NATE**
Members: **176**   Founded: **1995**

Barter Systems

4254 Gatecrest
San Antonio TX
78217 USA
Contact: Bob McLaren
  Phone: 210-650-9300
    Fax: 210-650-9044
  E Mail:
  Organ.: **NATE**
Members: **500**   Founded: **1983**

Barter Systems

Shartz TX
78154 USA
Contact: Rachel Taylor
  Phone: 210-651-9300
    Fax: 210-651-5434
  E Mail:
  Organ.: **NATE**
Members: Founded:

BXI Austin

4800 Broken Bow Pass
Austin TX
78745 USA
Contact: Bob Allen
  Phone: 512-282-4289
    Fax:
  E Mail:
  Organ.: **IRTA**
Members: Founded:

BXI Southwest

2351 W. NW Hwy. #2320
Dallas TX
75220 USA
Contact: Thomas Austin
  Phone: 214-350-6282
    Fax: 214-350-4757
  E Mail:
  Organ.: **IRTA**
Members: Founded:

ITEX Austin & BEI Holdings

1120 Capitol of Texas Hwy S.
Austin TX
78746 USA
Contact: Matthew O'Hayer
  Phone: 512-329-7250
    Fax: 512-329-7278
  E Mail:
  Organ.:
Members: Founded:

ITEX Corpus Christi

7150 Windobrook Ln.
Corpus Christi TX
78414 USA
Contact: Noma Perez
  Phone: 512-992-2558
    Fax: 512-992-2559
  E Mail:
  Organ.: **IRTA**
Members: Founded:

Merchant Trade, Inc

345 Owen Lane, Ste. 125
Waco TX
76710 USA
Contact: Bryon Lester
  Phone: 817-776-5552
    Fax: 817-772-5188
  E Mail:
  Organ.: **NATE**
Members: **500**   Founded: **1981**

Trade USA

5740 Prospect Ave.
Dallas TX
75206 USA
Contact: Bob Wilber
  Phone: 214-828-4324
    Fax: 214-828-0922
  E Mail:
  Organ.: **NATE**
Members: Founded: **1991**

VIRGINIA

Cybertrade

5605 Sedgemoor Rd.
Virginia Beach VA
23455 USA
Contact: Vic Shunkwiler
  Phone: 804-456-2597
    Fax: 804-463-2826
  E Mail:
  Organ.: **IRTA**
Members: Founded:

International Reciprocal Trade Association - IRTA

6305 Hawaii Court
Alexandria VA
22312 USA
Contact: Paul Suplizio
  Phone: 703-916-9020
    Fax: 703-914-9677
  E Mail: irta@dgsys.com
  Organ.: **IRTA**
Members: **180**   Founded: **1979**

VERMONT

Olde Vermont Trading Company

Box 191
West Dover VT
05356 USA
Contact: Marc Albano
  Phone: 802-464-2177
    Fax: 802-464-3809
  E Mail:
  Organ.: **IRTA**
Members: Founded:

Vermont Barter Network, Inc.
Box 746
Milton VT
05468 USA
Contact: William A. Burnett
Phone: 802-893-7557
Fax: 802-893-1446
E Mail:
Organ.: **IRTA**
Members: Founded: **1990**

Cascade Trade Association, Inc.
21400 Int'l. Blvd. Ste 207
Seattle   WA
98198-6086 USA
Contact: Steve White
Phone: 206-870-9290
Fax: 206-878-7224
E Mail:
Organ.: **NATE**
Members: **700**   Founded: **1983**

ITEX Spokane
N. 6619 Cedar Unit 101
Spokane WA
99208-4381 USA
Contact: Mark H. Ashburn
Phone: 509-328-5200
Fax: 509-328-5105
E Mail:
Organ.: **IRTA**
Members: Founded:

Continental Trade Exchange, ltd
Box 51305
New Berlin WI
53151-0305 USA
Contact: Don Mardak
Phone: 414-780-3640
Fax: 414-780-3655
E Mail:
Organ.: **NATE**
Members: Founded: **1985**

Rose Barter Group
N6261 HIghway East
Plymouth WI
53073 USA
Contact: Hans D. Rose
Phone: 414-893-6481
Fax: 414-892-6720
E Mail:
Organ.: **NATE**
Members: Founded:

Wisconsin Barter Exchange Corporation
1213 Frisch Rd.
Madison WI
53711 USA
Contact: Scott Sanftleben
Phone: 608-277-5999
Fax: 608-277-5996
E Mail:
Organ.: **IRTA NATE**
Members: **200**   Founded: **1994**

International Barter Organizations

(This is not a complete listing, but rather a sampling)

ARGENTINA

Barter Finance Group

Castex 3345, Piso 23°
Buenos Aires
1435 Argentina
Contact: Daniel Lew
Phone: 541-801-7400
Fax:
E Mail:
Organ.: **IRTA**
Members: Founded:

AUSTRALIA

Business Barter Exchange

Box 667
Hornsby NSW
2077 Australia
Contact: Michael Touma
Phone: 612-4766655
Fax: 612-4766402
E Mail:
Organ.: **IRTA**
Members: Founded:

Contra Card

105 Fern St.
Islington NSW
2010 Australia
Contact: Mark Pryke
Phone: 6149-623577
Fax: 6149-623717
E Mail:
Organ.: **IRTA**
Members: Founded:

International Business Exchange LTD

Southport Queensland
4215 Australia
Contact: Barrie Devenport
Phone: 61-75-916-000
Fax: 61-75-912-561
E Mail:
Organ.: **NATE**
Members: Founded:

The Queensland Trade Exchange

Unit 4 The Upton Centre 65
Bundall   QUE
4217 Australia
Contact: John Attridge
Phone: 075-925544
Fax: 075-924263
E Mail:
Organ.: **IRTA**
Members: Founded: **1990**

Tradebanc International PTY LTD

Suite 3/4 19 Restwell St.
Bankstown NSW
2200 Australia
Contact: Bill Rorke
  Phone: 612-796-4411
    Fax: 612-796-4442
  E Mail:
  Organ.: **IRTA**
Members: Founded: **1992**

Tradelink Barter

239 Scott Parade
Ballarat VIC
3350 Australia
Contact: Jim Walsh
  Phone: 6153-333955
    Fax: 6153-333885
  E Mail: mwalsh@netconnect.co
  Organ.: **IRTA**
Members: Founded:

BELGUIM

Unit Trade

Se Neufstraat 22-24 B-2100
Deurne-antwerp
Belguim
Contact: Peter Nauwelaerts
  Phone: 32-3326-5031
    Fax: 32-3326-2923
  E Mail:
  Organ.: **IRTA**
Members: Founded:

CANADA

ABC Canada Barter Connection Inc.

3332 Riverside Dr.
Ottawa, Ontario
K1V 8P1 Canada
Contact: Jane Darling Mullen
  Phone: 613-731-7283
    Fax: 613-731-7339
  E Mail:
  Organ.: **NATE**
Members: **3,000**   Founded: **1989**

Barter Business Exchange

1 Yorkdale Rd. #209
Toronto ONT
M6A 3A1 Canada
Contact: Robin Maini
  Phone: 416-782-3000
    Fax: 416-782-7438
  E Mail:
  Organ.: **IRTA NATE**
Members: **2,500**   Founded: **1991**

Barter Business Exchange Vancouver

1070 Ridgeway Ave #203
Coquitlam BC
V3J 1S7 Canada
Contact: Bill Jeffrey
  Phone: 604-936-4442
    Fax: 604-936-4461
  E Mail:
  Organ.: **NATE**
Members: Founded:

Barternet

456 Norte Dame Ave. #2
Winnipeg MAN
R3B 1R5 Canada
Contact: Don Parks
  Phone: 204-943-3953
    Fax: 204-943-6753
  E Mail:
  Organ.: **IRTA**
Members: Founded:

COMTEX Trade Exchange

1000 De La Montagne
Montreal QUE
H3G 1Y7 Canada
Contact: Herbert W. Teichmann
  Phone: 514-938-1234
    Fax: 514-938-4321
  E Mail:
  Organ.: **IRTA**
Members: Founded:

Barterplus Systems Inc

2 Lansing Sq, #804
North York ONT
M23 4P8 Canada
Contact: Michael Caron
  Phone: 416-490-9599
    Fax: 416-490-9377
  E Mail:
  Organ.: **IRTA NATE**
Members: **2,500**   Founded: **1991**

Genesis & Associates

Box 130
Durham, Ontario
N0G 1R0 Canada
Contact: George Benninger
  Phone: 519-369-6950
    Fax: 519-369-6961
  E Mail:
  Organ.: **NATE**
Members: Founded:

Caribbean Trade Exchange

61 Tecumseth St.
Toronto ON.
M5V 2X6 Canada
Contact: Peter Tucker
  Phone: 416-504-8925
    Fax: 416-504-7732
  E Mail:
  Organ.: **NATE**
Members: Founded:

Nationwide Barter Corporation

200 Ronson Dr., Ste. 102
Toronto ONT
M9W 5Z9 Canada
Contact: Larry Longo
  Phone: 416-249-8181
    Fax: 416-242-6468
  E Mail:
  Organ.: **IRTA**
Members: Founded:

Trade Barter Exchange
4 Meadowview Rd.
London ONT
N6J 4E6 Canada
Contact: John Cooper
Phone: 519-686-2747
Fax: 519-686-7915
E Mail:
Organ.: **IRTA**
Members: Founded:

BarterLink
Calle 75 No 13-51 Oficina 409
Bogota
Columbia
Contact: Alfredo Ramos
Phone: 571-310-1959
Fax: 571-616-2029
E Mail:
Organ.: **IRTA NATE**
Members: Founded: **1993**

Trading & Compensation
47 Rue de Chaillot
Paris
75116 France
Contact: Pascal Alexandre
Phone: 331-53232525
Fax: 331-47204414
E Mail:
Organ.: **IRTA**
Members: Founded:

Nordic Barter
Box 8602
Reykjavik
128 Iceland
Contact: Lúdvig Á. Sveinsson
Phone: 354-568-3870
Fax: 354-568-3875
E Mail:
Organ.: **IRTA**
Members: Founded:

Mexican Barter Association
3445 Catalina Dr.
Carlsbad CA
92008 México
Contact: Kirk Whisler
Phone: 619-433-0090
Fax: 619-433-0197
E Mail: mexico@deltanet.com
Organ.: **NATE**
Members: Founded: **1996**

Barter Trade International
Stradhoouderskade 2
Amsterdam
1054 Netherlands
Contact: Paul Logchies
Phone: 3120-6129661
Fax: 3120-6836650
E Mail:
Organ.: **IRTA**
Members: Founded:

NEW ZEALAND

Bartercard New Zealand
Box 8485 Symonds St.
Aukland
New Zealand
Contact: Wayne Sharpe
Phone: 649-309-0890
Fax: 649-309-0842
E Mail:
Organ.: IRTA
Members: Founded: 1991

SCOTLAND

The Bartering Company-Scotland
Suite 114 John Player Bldg.
Stirling
FK77RP Scotland
Contact: Mike Nasa
Phone: 44-1786-463214
Fax: 44-1786-447604
E Mail:
Organ.: IRTA
Members: Founded:

The Business Exhcange
77 Grampian Rd.
Abordeen
AB1 3ED Scotland
Contact: Linda Sim
Phone: 44-224-899077
Fax: 44-224-890244
E Mail:
Organ.: IRTA
Members: Founded:

SOUTH AFRICA

ITEX South Africa
Box 7898 Transvall
Johannesbury
2000 South Africa
Contact:
Phone: 2711-786-5433
Fax: 2711-887-1270
E Mail:
Organ.: IRTA
Members: Founded:

TURKEY

Ihlas Barter Organization A.S.
Ihlas 2 Han Cagloglu
Istanbul
0090 Turkey
Contact: Cemil Aral
Phone: 212-511-8950
Fax: 212-511-4138
E Mail:
Organ.: IRTA
Members: Founded:

UNITED KINGDOM

Barter International Group
1 Lumley Street-Mayfair
London
W1Y 1TW U.K.
Contact: Nicolas Loufrani
Phone: 44-171-493-4974
Fax: 44-171-408-2435
E Mail:
Organ.: IRTA
Members: Founded:

Business Barter Exchange

31 Tower Bridge Rd.
London
SE14TL U.K.
Contact: Ike Kahn
Phone: 44171-357-0808
Fax: 44171-357-0606
E Mail:
Organ.: **IRTA**
Members: Founded:

Eurotrade Business Barter Network

29 Brenkley Way Blezard
Newcastle
NE13 U.K.
Contact: Anthony Craggs
Phone: 4491-2170340
Fax: 4491-2170342
E Mail:
Organ.: **IRTA**
Members: Founded:

Executive Trade Exchange

4 Maguire St. Butler's Wharf
London
SE1 2NQ U.K.
Contact: Ravin Bhavnani
Phone: 44-171-572-1050
Fax: 44-171-572-1040
E Mail:
Organ.: **IRTA**
Members: Founded:

ICM, Ltd.

75 Gresham Rd.
Staines Middlesex
TW18 2BH U.K.
Contact: Michael Timoney
Phone: 441784-466899
Fax: 441784-457212
E Mail:
Organ.: **IRTA**
Members: Founded:

Media Resources International U.K. Ltd.

No. 10 Jamestown Rd. Camden
London
NW1 7BY U.K.
Contact: Simon Lee
Phone: 44141-4282888
Fax: 44171-4825657
E Mail:
Organ.: **IRTA**
Members: Founded:

Orion Gold Barter Corp

Shirley Lodge 470 London Rd.
Slough, Bershire
SL3 8QY U.K.
Contact: Mark Pearse
Phone: 44-1753-540550
Fax: 44-1753-540560
E Mail:
Organ.: **IRTA**
Members: Founded:

The Bartering Company - Channel Islands

Box 211 74 Stopford Rd.
St. Helier Jersey
JE4 8SZ U.K.
Contact: K.M. Rondel
Phone: 44-534-69137
Fax: 44-534-27773
E Mail:
Organ.: **IRTA**
Members: Founded:

URUGUAY

BC Barter Uruguay

Ing. Garcia de Zuniga 2245/1104
Montevideo
CP11300 Uruguay
Contact: Leo Dibueno
Phone: 5982-712-862
Fax: 5982-910-656
E Mail:
Organ.: **IRTA**
Members: Founded:

United States Corporate Barter Organizations

(This is not a complete listing, but rather a sampling)

CALIFORNIA

Merchant's Exchange
2838 University Av. #103-244
San Diego CA
92104 USA
Contact: Jane Goei
Phone: 619-460-1090
Fax: 619-460-1160
E Mail:
Organ.:
Members: 160   Founded: 1992

CONNECTICUT

Stephen L. Geller, Inc (SLG)
2 Greenwich Office Park
Greenwich CT
06830 USA
Contact: Mary Ann Shraky
Phone: 203-622-6669
Fax: 203-622-8885
E Mail:
Organ.:
Members: Founded:

GEORGIA

Media Exchange, Inc.
5505 Roswell Rd. #350
Atlanta GA
30342 USA
Contact: Bette Bryman
Phone: 404-256-2034
Fax: 404-256-2614
E Mail:
Organ.: IRTA
Members: Founded: 1985

ILLINOIS

U. S. Intermark
900 North Shore Dr.
Lake Bluff IL
60044 USA
Contact: Robert Rosenstiel
Phone: 847-735-8723
Fax: 847-735-8727
E Mail:
Organ.: IRTA
Members: Founded: 1979

NEW YORK

Active International

1 Blue Hill Plaza, 9th Floor
Pearl River NY
10965 USA
Contact: Alan Elkin
  Phone: 914-735-1700
    Fax: 914-735-7665
  E Mail: aelkin@active.mhs.com
  Organ.: **IRTA**
Members: Founded: **1984**

American Marketing Complex

4 Park Ave. Ste. 9 E
New York NY
10016 USA
Contact: Norman King
  Phone: 212-355-4700
    Fax:
  E Mail:
  Organ.:
Members: Founded:

Broadcast Marketing

1633 Broadway
New York NY
10019 USA
Contact: Diane Dunbar
  Phone: 212-424-9247
    Fax: 212-246-7476
  E Mail:
  Organ.:
Members: Founded:

CSI International

800 2nd Ave.
New York NY
10017 USA
Contact: William Schachter
  Phone: 212-687-5600
    Fax: 212-867-6113
  E Mail:
  Organ.:
Members: Founded: **1979**

Global Marketing Resources

360 Madison Ave.
New York NY
10017 USA
Contact: Mike Suscavage
  Phone: 212-297-0000
    Fax: 212-297-0073
  E Mail:
  Organ.: **IRTA**
Members: Founded: **1991**

Icon International

220 E. 42nd St #1601
New York NY
10017 USA
Contact: Lance Lundburg
  Phone: 212-972-7373
    Fax: 212-972-3366
  E Mail:
  Organ.:
Members: Founded: **1985**

Kent Trading, Inc.
600 Madison Ave.
New York NY
10022 USA
Contact: Robert Klein
  Phone: 212-371-5225
    Fax: 212-752-6594
  E Mail: bobk@mediabuying.com
  Organ.:
Members: Founded: **1985**

Media Resources International
275 Madison Ave. 4th Fl.
New York NY
10016 USA
Contact: Peter Benassi
  Phone: 212-557-7575
    Fax: 212-557-7574
  E Mail:
  Organ.:
Members: Founded: **1991**

Lakeside Group Inc.
210 E. 39th
New York NY
10016 USA
Contact: Fred Tarter
  Phone: 212-679-3800
    Fax: 212-679-3816
  E Mail:
  Organ.:
Members: Founded: **1970**

RTE, Inc.
1595 Elmwood Av.
Rochester NY
14620 USA
Contact: Stephen E. Webster
  Phone: 716-244-0600
    Fax: 716-244-9042
  E Mail:
  Organ.: **NATE**
Members: **1,500**   Founded: **1978**

Media Barter Associates
150 E. 58th St.
New York NY
10155 USA
Contact: Harold Commings
  Phone: 212-750-5400
    Fax: 212-750-5823
  E Mail:
  Organ.:
Members: Founded:

S.G.D. Int'l.
360 West 253 St.
Riverdale NY
10471 USA
Contact: Jerry Galuten
  Phone: 212-265-9000
    Fax: 718-601-8059
  E Mail:
  Organ.:
Members: **750**   Founded: **1980**

The Intrac Group
424 Madison Ave.
New York NY
10019-6102 USA
Contact: Thomas A. Settineri
  Phone: 212-247-2300
    Fax: 212-247-5851
  E Mail:
  Organ.: **IRTA**
Members: Founded: **1991**

Tradewell Inc.
845 Third Ave. 16th Fl
New York NY
10022 USA
Contact: William S. Steinberg
  Phone: 212-888-8500
    Fax: 212-755-6312
  E Mail:
  Organ.:
Members: Founded: **1977**

Warner Media Inc.
114 E. 32nd St. Ste. 404
New York NY
10016 USA
Contact: Erwin Rosner
  Phone: 212-447-5900
    Fax: 212-447-5973
  E Mail:
  Organ.:
Members: Founded: **1954**

Woolworth Corporation
233 Broadway
New York NY
10279-0003 USA
Contact: Donald A. Lyon
  Phone: 212-553-2319
    Fax: 212-553-2495
  E Mail:
  Organ.:
Members: Founded:

OHIO

Tradecorp
707 Enterprise
Columbus OH
43801 USA
Contact: Art Goehring
  Phone: 614-846-4041
    Fax: 614-436-8490
  E Mail:
  Organ.: **NATE**
Members: **2,000**   Founded: **1976**

TEXAS

Inventory Merchandising Services
1120 Capitol of Texas Hwy.
Austin TX
78746 USA
Contact: Tim Valintine
  Phone: 512-329-7250
    Fax: 512-329-7278
  E Mail:
  Organ.: **IRTA**
Members: **500**   Founded: **1982**

VIRGINIA

ITEX USA Inc.
321 Greenhill St.
Great Falls VA
22066 USA
Contact: Clyde Fabretti
Phone: 703-757-5100
Fax: 703-757-5121
E Mail:
Organ.: **IRTA**
Members: Founded:

National Countertrade Corporation
1300 Lafayette Dr., #200
Alexandria VA
22308 USA
Contact: F. Lowell Curtis
Phone: 703-765-5500
Fax: 703-765-5503
E Mail: www.erols.com/acer75/
Organ.: **IRTA NATE**
Members: **500**   Founded: **1981**

International Reciprocal Trade Association

Your Entre to Reliable Commercial Barter Companies Worldwide

Who We Are

IRTA is a non-profit association chartered in the U.S.A. Our members are 175 barter companies located predominantly in North America but also in Great Britain, France, Belgium, Holland, Iceland, Australia, New Zealand, South Africa, Colombia, and Argentina who subscribe to our Code of Ethics and a peer review self-regulatory system. Our member trade exchanges facilitate barter purchase and sale of goods and services among small and medium size businesses. Our Corporate Trade Council comprises leading corporate barter companies who handle multi-million dollar transactions for domestic and multinational firms.

What We Do

IRTA's mission is to uphold a strong Code of Ethics for the barter industry and raise the value of barter services to the business community.

- We are a point of contact for businesses wanting to learn more about barter and meet reputable barter companies.

- We are pioneering Bartercom, a global electronic exchange network of products and services available on barter. Visit us on the Internet at http://www2.dgsys.com/~irta/, E-Mail: irta@dgsys.com. For further information, send a stamped self-addressed envelope to IRTA, 6305 Hawaii Court, Alexandria, VA 22312.

BUSINESS
IS A GAME THAT NEVER ENDS

BARTER BUSINESS
E X C H A N G E

TORONTO • WINDSOR • VANCOUVER • HAMILTON

BBE is a member of the National Association of Trade Exchanges and the Better Business Bureau

Maybe You Need a Barter Strategy...

In today's roller-coaster economy, your restaurant often has to spend more than it takes in.

You're not alone.

Spiralling overhead, tight cash flow and shrinking margins are causing companies to rethink their cash management strategies for the 90's.

That's why companies of all sizes and in every service category are discovering the advantages of using barter to improve cash flow and reduce excess inventory.

Bartering for the goods and services your restaurant needs is an effective management tool that goes straight to the bottom line and makes good financial sense.

What is Barter Business Exchange?

BBE is Canada's largest barter exchange, with thousands of active members trading for goods and services that you're probably paying cash for right now.

BBE manages all trading activities and helps source what your business needs, while at the same time promoting what your business can trade to other members.

Isn't it time your restaurant strengthened its buying power with a barter strategy?

For more information or a free informative brochure and video of goods and services available on the exchange, call Barter Business Exchange today:

1-800-994-0041
(416) 782-3000

CHEQUEMATE!

BARTER BUSINESS
E X C H A N G E

BBE is a member of the National Association of Trade Exchanges and the IRTA

Why write a cheque when you can improve your cash flow position with barter?

In today's roller-coaster economic climate your business often has to spend more than it takes in.

You're not alone.

Spiralling overhead and tight cash flow are causing companies to rethink their cash management strategies for the 90's.

That's why companies of all sizes and in every business category are discovering the advantages of using barter to improve cash flow. Bartering for the goods and services your company needs is an effective management tool that goes straight to the bottom line and makes good financial sense.

What is Barter Business Exchange?

BBE is Canada's fastest growing barter exchange with over 1,000 active members trading for goods and services that you're probably paying cash for right now.

BBE manages all trading activities and helps source what your business needs, while at the same time promoting what your business can trade to other members.

Isn't it time your business strengthened its cash flow position with a barter strategy?

For more information or a free informative brochure and listing of goods and services available on the exchange call Barter Business Exchange today at:

(416) 782-3000
1-800-994-0041

Things just couldn't be better.
(or could they?)

It's great!
You finally own your own business and YOU are the boss. But a
tight cash flow can be a tough hurdle in your fledgling years.
And, you can always use more business to help ends meet.

B A R T E R
does just that.

Discover how you
can pay for your
expenses with your
product or service,
instead of cash.

*Barter, the cash
alternative.*

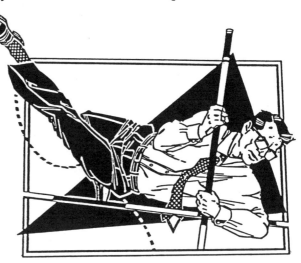

Stay On Top Of The Game - Contact Us For:
A List Trade Exchanges In Your Area
Information On How To Start A Trade Exchange
Additional Details About Barter

National Association
of Trade Exchanges

T H R E E Easy Ways
Phone: 216-732-7171
Fax: 216-732-7172
Mail: 27801 Euclid - #610
Cleveland OH   44132

Now you can trade
in Canada
3000

CANADA

*W*ith more than 3000 members coast-to-coast, ABC Canada offers you the largest selection of businesses, products and services from the largest trade network in Canada.

*W*hy settle for less?

*F*or a membership and your own personal ABC Canada members directory, send **$99** plus 7% GST (if applicable) by cheque or money order made payable to:

ABC Canada
a div. of Barter Connection Inc.
3332 Riverside Drive
Ottawa, Ontario, Canada
K1V 8P1

VISA

Use your Visa and have your order processed immediately. Call now

1•800•361•8801 In Canada
1•613•731•7283 Outside of Canada

FREE

For more information
complete the form
and FAX to
(613) 731-7339

coast-to-coast
with more than
businesses and
it's as easy as

ABC

I'll Take Manhattan?

For thousands of years men and women have traded their goods and services. Cloth for spices. Tobacco for weapons. Horses for a big bag of hot bagels with lox and cream cheese.

But in 1626 Dutch settlers in the New World made the most bodacious barter deal in history. For beaded necklaces, a bag o' shells and other nameless wampum, they purchased the entire island of Manhattan.* You too can make barter a rewarding part of your business. Trade for the services you need instead of spending cash.

Call today to see how **Allied Barter** can help expand your business opportunities and improve your cash flow...

NOW there's a better way

Allied Barter
corporation℠

4830 43rd Street, NW
Washington, DC 20016

202-364-4ABC

*Sorry, Manhattan is not available for barter at the moment. But no matter. Many tourists, after visiting New York City believe it was the Dutch who were left holding the bag.

America's Barter Network

A COMMON LAW BUSINESS TRUST

in·ter·na·tion·al (in'tər-nash'ə-nəl) *adj.* Of, relating to, or involving two or more nations or nationalities.

bar·ter (bär'tər) *v.* To trade (e.g. goods or services) without using money.

group (grōop) *n.* A number of persons or things (e.g. businesses) gathered, located, or classified together.

THE PUBLISHERS OF
101 WAYS TO GROW
YOUR BUSINESS WITH BARTER
WOULD LIKE YOU TO LOOK
FOR THESE OTHER WPR BOOKS

STEPPING STONES TO SUCCESS SERIES

101 Ways To Improve Your Marketing Efforts To Hispanics. By Zeke Montes, Kirk Whisler, and Katherine A. Díaz. Comprehensive marketing book on how to more effectively reach the rapidly growing Hispanic market in the United States. $16.95.

The Hispanic Scholarship Directory. Edited by Andrés Tobar and others and published with the National Association of Hispanic Publications. A directory of over 500 scholarships available to Hispanic students in the United States and international students from Latin America. $19.95.

MARKETING GUIDEPOST SERIES

The 1997 National Hispanic Media Directory. By Kirk Whisler and Octavio Nuiry. Profiles over 1,600 Hispanic publications, TV stations, radio stations, ad agencies, public relations firms and internet operators. Published with ADR Publishing. $95.00.

The National Hispanic Readership Profile. By Dr. Leobardo F. Estrada. The results of the first comprehensive national study of readers of Hispanic publications in the United States. $19.95.

FUTURE TITLES IN THE FOLLOWING SERIES WILL BE AVAILABLE SOON:

DOCUMENTING ACHIEVEMENTS

CHILDREN

HEALTH

TRAVEL

The Mexican Barter Association

After a year of solid planning and preparation, *Asociación Mexicana de Intercambios S.A. de C.V.* (Mexican Barter Association) is proud to have started full time operations in June 1996

THE ORGANIZATION IS CURRENTLY SEEKING APPROPRIATE INTERNATIONAL TRADES

For more information please write the
United States office at
3445 Catalina Dr.
Carlsbad, California 92008
or phone 619-433-0090

WE LOOK FORWARD TO WORKING WITH YOU

Helping normal businesses involved in barter to better use barter as a marketing and cash management tool.

Focusing on the retail and exchange portions of the barter industry.

Articles about direct business to business trading and trading involving the use of trade credits.

North American Barter™

The Who, What, When, Where, Why & How of Barter

Learn how to expand

your business and

conserve

valuable

cash by

bartering.

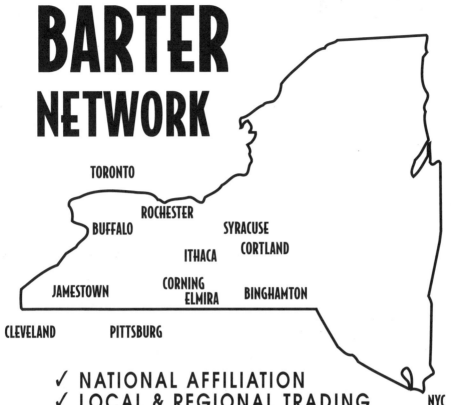

BUSINESS OWNERS...
Announcing a New Generation of Credit Card:

The *Trade Card*™
from TCE

*If you're not using the
Trade Card™ from TCE,
you're missing out on
the exciting multi-billion
dollar Barter industry!*

BARTER - THE MULTI-BILLION DOLLAR INDUSTRY

The Barter Concept is as old as man. Cash was originally invented as a convenient substitute for Barter. Since the TEFRA Act passed congress in 1984, Barter organizations have been recognized by the Federal Government and the IRS as third-party record keepers, along with banks, insurance companies and stock brokerages.

Government and Fortune 500 companies have Bartered for many years. Now, with the *Trade Card*™ from TCE, so can your company.

HOW THE *TRADE CARD*™ FROM TCE WORKS

Trade Club Exchange is a network of thousands of business owners and professionals who have formed a Barter organization to the mutual benefit of all members. *(We're doing more business!)*

TCE Members sell their goods and services through the exchange and earn Trade Dollars, which are credited to their trade account and used to purchase from other exchange members.

Purchases are made using the *Trade Card*™ from TCE and "trade vouchers," just like any other credit card. TCE acts as a third party record keeper and handles all accounting procedures. Members are issued a regular monthly statement which itemizes their trade transactions for the month.

This system is similar to major credit card companies, but unlike these companies, TCE brings you new business, new customers, new sales and greater profits. And, also unlike the conventional credit card companies, TCE earns its percentages from the buyer, not the merchant.

BUILD YOUR BOTTOM LINE

Trade Club Exchange is one of the fastest growing Barter organizations in the nation today. Thousands of business owners and professionals have already joined TCE and are waiting to do business with you. Earn Trade Dollars from these new TCE customers and put your new purchasing power to work running your business, expanding your operation or enhancing your personal standard of living.

BRING IN NEW BUSINESS

In your local market and across the country, TCE builds your bottom line with new customers and more sales. Our members are dedicated to Barter and ready to do business with you. All TCE members are business owners and professionals who create an instant market for your business related products and services. These same people will also become a major market for your consumer products and personal services as they spend Trade Dollars to improve their style of living.

You may also use your Trade Dollars to advertise for more CA$H business. Turn your Trade Dollars into cash receipts by using any of the many advertising and printing related services in the organization to promote your business.

And, TCE can help you find new Barter business with media and advertising like the TCE Barter Pages Directory, the monthly Photo Trader Directory supplements and Direct Mail Programs.

UNLOCK FROZEN ASSETS

Build up your bottom line by unlocking your frozen assets. Put your excess production / service time or unsold inventory to work for you. You cannot bill tomorrow for goods or services unsold today. TCE has buyers waiting and will help you earn Trade Dollars which you may then spend on business or personal needs.

CONSERVE YOUR CASH

TCE offers you an easy way to build your bottom line by offsetting your cash expenses. _STOP_ spending your cash - start spending TCE Trade Dollars! Are you spending cash for any of these items?

- Advertising
- Accounting
- Incentives
- Automotive Upkeep
- Entertainment
- Legal Services
- Medical/Dental
- Maintenance/Janitorial

Use your TCE Trade Dollars to cover many of your business expenses or personal needs. Put your hard-earned cash in the bank! You benefit from a stronger cash position, making money available when you need it.

Every TCE Trade Dollar you spend can represent a cash dollar in the bank. Use TCE to conserve your vital cash flow and dramatically improve your bottom line.

TCE's INTELLIGENT MULTI-LEVEL CONCEPT

TCE's Multi-Level sponsoring concept has reduced the customary $500 to $1,200 membership fee that other Barter organizations charge to only $178 for your first year's annual cash dues and a New Member Supply Kit. This kit includes an informative video, your _Trade Card™_ from TCE and everything you need to get started trading with TCE…_PLUS, a 30 day money-back guarantee!_

How is that possible? It's simple! Here's how it works:

Other exchanges employ a sales staff to bring members into the organization, which adds to the administration cost and is passed along to the membership as initiation fees and monthly dues.

TCE, however, has no need to hire costly salespeople. Our members ARE our sales force. So, we pass the SAVINGS along to you!

Another plus: The more members you bring into the club, the more opportunities you have to profit, both by using their goods and services, _and_ by a financial override on their trade volume.

WHY JOIN TRADE CLUB EXCHANGE

1. To fill sales voids by trading excess time and unsold or outdated inventory at, or close to, full value.
2. To generate new sales. TCE trade business is "new" business, in addition to your cash sales. It is business you would not normally receive. Sales are automatic - no member will spend cash if they can get it with their _Trade Card™._
3. To generate cash by using your Trade Dollars to advertise for additional cash customers.
4. To preserve cash flow to pay for non-trade operating costs (e.g., rent, electricity, telephones), by using TCE Trade Dollars on tradable overhead items (e.g., printing, accounting, advertising, etc.).
5. Generally, in a trade transaction there is more profit (i.e., fixed operating costs are already paid for with cash transactions). TCE trade customers mean new business and the proceeds can be used for other costs (both business and personal). As a result, hard earned cash dollars will stay in your pocket!
6. During tough times, the demand for trade business is at an all-time high. Sales voids are filled with trade business and new customers. Often trade makes the difference in business survival.
7. Trade representatives will assist you with spending and generating Trade Dollars.
8. To network with thousands of business owners at business expos, mixers and orientations.
9. As a member of the TCE network, you eliminate the challenges of one-to-one trading.

Call or write for more information:
TRADE CLUB EXCHANGE, INC.
7717 Garden Grove Blvd., Garden Grove CA 92641
(714) 891-8497 • FAX (714) 895-2895 • 1-800-643-4480

MULTI-LEVEL BARTER SYSTEM™

Hottest New Profit Center For Small Business

By J. R. Veem, Staff Reporter for S.D.B. Teller

Cash-hungry small companies are turning to history's 2nd oldest profession to fight off the economic slowdown.

Commercial trade exchanges (BARTER) are experiencing meteoric growth in the last decade according to Nelson B. Guyer, president and founder of San Diego Barter. More and more companies are discovering a viable *Secondary Profit Center* through retail reciprocal trade exchanges also known as BARTER Exchanges, according to Guyer.

Here's how it works:

■ **The Primary Profit Center**: Cash is good, spends anywhere and is highly recommended for any business. To the dismay of many small business owners, cash revenue does not always compute to profits. Cash profits from revenue are a function of what is left after deducting fixed and variable expenses. "Only after your *Primary Profit Center* is established, should you consider the *Secondary Profit Center*," admonished Guyer.

■ **The Secondary Profit Center**: If you're not doing 10-15% in Barter, according to the Harvard School of Business, "You're leaving money on the table." Profit margins tend to be much higher in the *Secondary Profit Center* because the only deduction from revenue is variable or incremental costs incurred. For example, the cost to a restaurant for extra business through a Barter Exchange is food & beverage. Rent, salaries, advertising and insurance are fixed and have already been paid.

■ **Your Benefits**: Expand your customer base, increase your profits and conserve cash. Do all this with new business while capturing a greater share of the market from your competitors.

■ **What do I get for the new business I deliver?** Trade Dollars (same as cash, according to IRS) indeed become "same as cash" as soon as these trade units or dollars are spent. P. S. You are not necessarily obligated to spend your trade dollars with the same new clients that bought from you.

■ **What is available?** Everything from painting to printing, recreation to inspiration and forklifts to facelifts. One of our clients recently requested a dating service. As a result we now feature "honies" and "hunks" in our vast inventory of products and services, says Mr. Guyer of S. D. B.

■ **Your Costs:** Most barter exchanges have a modest initiation and monthly administration fee. Typically, exchanges handle recordkeeping, expedite the flow of trades and promote clients through directories and newsletters. In return they take a 10-15% slice off the top of each transaction.

■ **Should I consider the *Secondary Profit Center* for my business?** For a free, no obligation feasibility study (it doesn't work for every business) CALL N. B. Guyer @ The San Diego Barter corporate office 619) 587-3938.

A New World of Opportunity

You already know the benefits of barter. But to take full advantage and increase your bottom line, you need to position yourself with a leader. That's Tradecorp. Since 1976, we've been the largest quality trade exchange in the Midwest, ranking in the top 3% of all U.S. exchanges. Currently we provide over 2,000 clients with access to over 50,000 trading businesses throughout the country. And our personal brokers are available 24 hours a day, 7 days a week. Discover how we can provide a new world of opportunities for your business. Contact Tradecorp today.

Tradecorp Barter Excellence Since 1976

Green Meadows Corporate Park
707 Enterprise Drive
Westerville, Ohio 43081
(614) 846-4041
Fax (614) 436-8490

U. S. INTERMARK, INC.

TRADE MARKETING
CONSULTANTS

- U. S. INTERMARK IS A PROFESSIONAL TRADE CONSULTING AND TRADE MARKETING FIRM FOUNDED IN 1979.

- U S I PROVIDES EXPERTISE AND SERVICES TO MAJOR CORPORATIONS IN THE FIELD OF CORPORATE TRADE AND INTERNATIONAL COUNTERTRADE.

- U S I BELONGS TO VARIOUS PROFESSIONAL TRADE ASSOCIATIONS, INCLUDING THE INTERNATIONAL RECIPROCAL TRADE ASSOCIATION.

SINCE 1979

FOR RESUME OF SERVICES OFFERED
CALL 847-735-8273
FAX 847-735-8727

900 NORTH SHORE DRIVE, SUITE 190 • LAKE BLUFF, IL 60044

KIRK WHISLER

Bartering is something that Kirk has actively practiced since he traded baseball cards at Del Rosa Elementary School in San Bernardino. In 1996 he was one of the founding directors of Asociación Mexicana de Intercambios S.A. de C.V.–the Mexican Barter Association.

Since 1992 Kirk Whisler has served as publisher of *MEXICO Events & Destinations* Magazine. Between 1986 and 1992 Kirk was publisher of NEVADA Magazine. From 1977 to 1986 Kirk was publisher of *SOMOS* and *CAMINOS* Magazines.

In 1982 Kirk was chosen as the founding president of the National Association of Hispanic Publications, the largest trade association of its kind. Since 1983 Kirk has been the publisher of The National Hispanic Media Directory.

Kirk is married to Magdalena González Whisler and together they are the proud parents of Spencer Diego (eight years old), Tito Andrés (six), and Zeke Emilio (five).

JIM SULLIVAN

As national sales director for *MEXICO Events & Destinations* Magazine for the past 4 years, Jim has dealt with hotels and tourism departments all over Mexico. The economic realities of those clients forced Jim to adopt a more creative approach to ad sales. Adding the element of barter to his presentations has resulted in considerably more ad pages for the magazine as well as a large inventory of travel.

Jim spent 5 years as sales director/general manger of a Spanish language TV guide in Houston. In 1986 Jim left his native southern California to be the sales director for a firm in New York City representing the National Association of Hispanic Publications.

Before getting into advertising sales in 1978, Jim ran his own English pub in San Bernardino, California and played on the professional dart circuit for ten years.

Jim is a proud Vietnam veteran, and is currently single.

THE PUBLISHERS OF
101 WAYS TO GROW YOUR BUSINESS WITH BARTER
WOULD LIKE YOU TO LOOK FOR THESE OTHER WPR BOOKS

STEPPING STONES TO SUCCESS SERIES

101 Ways To Improve Your Marketing Efforts To Hispanics. By Zeke Montes, Kirk Whisler, and Katherine A. Díaz. Comprehensive marketing book on how to more effectively reach the rapidly growing Hispanic market in the United States. $16.95.

The Hispanic Scholarship Directory. Edited by Andrés Tobar and others and published with the National Association of Hispanic Publications. A directory of over 500 scholarships available to Hispanic students in the United States and international students from Latin America. $19.95.

MARKETING GUIDEPOST SERIES

The 1997 National Hispanic Media Directory. By Kirk Whisler and Octavio Nuiry. Profiles over 1,600 Hispanic publications, TV stations, radio stations, ad agencies, public relations firms and internet operators. Published with ADR Publishing. $95.00.

The National Hispanic Readership Profile. By Dr. Leobardo F. Estrada. The results of the first comprehensive national study of readers of Hispanic publications in the United States. $19.95.

FUTURE TITLES IN THE FOLLOWING SERIES WILL BE AVAILABLE SOON:

DOCUMENTING ACHIEVEMENTS

CHILDREN

HEALTH

TRAVEL

INDEX